Thank you

To my incredible, encouraging, and beautiful wife Jenny, your love and support made the writing of this book possible, you are a gift from God. I adore you. To my pastors and friends, Jürgen and Leanne Matthesius, thank you for not only believing in me, but constantly encouraging me, giving me opportunities to grow and challenging me with your examples of generosity, transparency, and love. To my parents Nick and Kathy, thank you for always encouraging me to think for myself, and for loving me through the most unlovable moments of my life. To my brother Garrett, thank you for all you are and all you have been to me, knowing that you were watching me has made me want to be a better man. To my children Ella and Jack, I look forward to seeing you grow, and growing with you through life, you have taught me to love in a far deeper way than I had imagined possible. To Jon and Becky Heinrichs, thank you for your example, for your faith, for bringing me up and for giving me opportunity to lead. Dr. Matt and Mikala Hubbard, thank you for your constant encouragement, for your prayers, for the opportunities you've given me and for keeping my family healthy physically and spiritually. To Tim Hall, thank you for stopping me on the street and telling me I need to write this book. To Kelli Hillard and Allison Armerding thank-you for continuing to challenge me not only to get this book finished, but challenging me to make it better along the way. To Pastor George Clerie, thank you for investing in me personally, for giving me a solid foundation, not just as a Christian, but as a man, a husband and a father. I wouldn't be where I am without your influence. To Mark, Will, Tyla and Nick, my sponsors and mentors in recovery, thank you for the countless hours you spent with me, your self-sacrifice, transparency and talking me off the ledge more times than I could count literally saved my life. To all my friends in recovery, in church, and in life, I love you. To Nick Henderson, you taught me the incredible freedom of forgiveness, and living a life without secrets—I wish you were alive to see this book, I hope you'd be proud of it. To Sevan Kevorkian, Axel Schoepflin, André Sobel and all of my friends that were lost to addiction. I love you, I miss you, this book is for you.

A journey from broken to breakthrough—discovering identity, overcoming addiction, and living free.

Morgan Ervin

Copyright © 2019 by Morgan Ervin

Printed in the United States of America

All rights reserved. No part of this publication may be reproduced, distributed, or transmitted in any form or by any means, including photocopying, recording, or other electronic or mechanical methods, without the prior written permission of the publisher, except in the case of brief quotations embodied in critical reviews and certain other noncommercial uses permitted by copyright law.

For permission requests, write to the publisher, with "Attention: Permissions Coordinator" in the subject line at the email address below.

Info@PowertoChangeBook.com

Quantity sales. Special discounts are available on quantity purchases by corporations, associations, and others. For details, contact publisher at the address above.

The Power to Change: A Journey From Broken To Breakthrough—Discovering Identity, Overcoming Addiction, and Living Free.

ISBN: 978-1-949709-72-8

All Scripture quotations, unless otherwise indicated, are taken from the Holy Bible, New International Version®. NIV®. Copyright © 1973, 1978, 1984 by International Bible Society. Used by permission of Zondervan. All rights reserved.

Italics in Scripture quotations reflect the author's emphasis.

Contents

Dedication	3
Introduction by Jurgen Matthesius	9
The Man in the Mirror	12
Chapter 1: Unusual is Normal When it's All That You Know	15
Chapter 2: Illegitimate Solutions to Legitimate Problems	27
Chapter 3: I'm Not the One Who's Going to Change Your Life	45
Chapter 4: The Bondage of Freedom	59
Chapter 5: No Matter Where You Go, There You Are	69
Chapter 6: Pride & Prejudice	85
Chapter 7: Power Tools	95
Chapter 8: Miracle Grow	107
Chapter 9: School for Fools	121
Chapter 10: You're Not All-In	131
Chapter 11: Love Letters to My Future Wife	143
Chapter 12: The Mission Field of My Heart	153
Chapter 13: A Unwanted Gift	165
Chapter 14: Faithful to Heal	173
Chapter 15: Planted to Grow	183
Chapter 16: Can You Grow a Beard?	195
Chapter 17: The Promise in the Process	201

Introduction

When I departed from the career path of becoming a mechanical engineer the major motivating factor was that we would spend months and sometimes years building steel products, only to load them into giant rectangular containers, and place them on cargo ships to be sent off to distant lands where we would never see them again. A shudder went through my soul—"Is this what my life will be like from now on? Working on projects never to see them again?!"

What I love about the gospel of Jesus Christ, is that it IS the POWER OF GOD unto salvation! (Romans 1:16) it became a very easy decision to go to bible school and see this Power change lives for the better week in and week out!

After 28 years of ministry spanning three nations, New Zealand, Australia and America one of the most beautiful stories of transformation I've encountered is that of Morgan Ervin. He perfectly illustrates the human condition of growing up in a broken world, dominated by a 'dog eat dog' and 'each man for himself' mindset where love, affection and development are priceless commodities enjoyed by a very select few.

Morgan, had an transformational moment with Jesus Christ that forever SHIFTED everything in his world view and life. It wasn't the discovery of religion it was an encounter with a risen savior who has the power to redeem, deliver, heal and transform!

This book, *The Power to Change* illustrates a truth that the devil has tried to bury in our generational life time. That is, that you DON'T HAVE TO ACCEPT ANYTHING LESS than what the Bible promises for your life! There is a truth that goes like this: "You cannot be delivered from something you consider normal!" The devil works overtime to normalize our sin, dysfunction & our dispositions. BUT the gospel is the GREAT INTERRUPTOR shattering the lies of the devil and freeing those who dare to believe that through God all things are possible!

Strap yourself in. Find a comfortable chair, and get ready, because as you begin to read this amazing true story, FAITH is going to rise on the inside of you and an opportunity to connect with the power of the risen savior will become apparent and before you're finished you will discover that Kansas will be going bye bye!

As Morgan's pastor and friend, I could not be more proud of him and could not be more excited to endorse the truths in this wonderful story. May God bless you as you read. May His glorious face shine upon you and His POWER overshadow you so that it transcends written literature and becomes a 'divine moment' of encounter and metamorphosis!

Jurgen Matthesius
Senior Pastor, C3 San Diego

The Power to Change

The Power to Change

MAY 20 1995:

The Man in the Mirror

Starbucks was especially busy that morning. It was the only one in my tourist-filled town back then, and we had just introduced Frappuccinos. I was stationed behind the espresso machine making drinks, and as the orders kept piling up, I was starting to panic. These were the days before we wrote the drink orders on cups—the cashier called them down the line and the baristas had to make them from memory. On a normal day—when I was sober—I had no problem keeping multiple orders straight. But only twelve hours had passed since I'd wrapped up a ten-day binge of smoking cocaine and drinking vodka, and I could feel that I was starting to detox. The coffee, orange juice, and water I had downed at the start of my shift certainly hadn't been enough to take the edge off my raging hangover.

All of I sudden, while staring at the nearly twenty paper cups lined up by the espresso machine, I realized that I couldn't remember a single drink order. My panic spiked and a tightness gripped my chest. Helplessly, I started to cry.

My manager, who had stepped in to help with the rush, called out another drink order. When I didn't respond, she looked over and saw me paralyzed with fear.

"I'll take care of the drinks, Morgan," she said. "Go ahead and brew some drip coffee."

Thankful to be rescued, but still panicking, I turned to perform the simple, low-stress task. I tried desperately to breathe and ignore my racing thoughts as I waited for the coffee to brew, but nothing helped. As I was transferring my first batch of coffee from the brewer to the warming plate, I began shaking uncontrollably. I dropped the pot on the floor, drenching myself and everything around me with 190-degree hot coffee.

Frantically, I ran to the back to look for burn gel, leaving my manager and one coworker to deal with my mess, the line out the door, and the long list of unmade drink orders.

About five minutes later, my manager came to confront me. She didn't need to remind me that I was on the verge of losing my job. I had already been written up for five infractions in the previous month—all caused by my drug and alcohol use. Yet every time she or others had called me out, I had stubbornly clung to the delusion that I didn't have a problem. Drugs and alcohol weren't my problem—they were the only things that helped me deal with my problems.

Yet now, my stubbornness was slipping. After listening to my manager's ultimatum that I could only keep my job if I got help, I ran to the employee bathroom to fall apart. I couldn't hold back the tears of frustration, anguish, and despair a minute longer.

At last, I picked myself off the floor and walked to the sink to wash my face. And it was in that moment, as I stared into the mirror, that my delusion broke, and the truth of who I had become finally struck me in full force.

I was nineteen-year-old alcoholic and drug addict.

How on earth did I end up here?

And more importantly, what was I going to do?

CHAPTER 1:
Unusual is Normal When it's All That You Know

I've never thought of my life as abnormal. I didn't assume other people must be having the same experiences as me—I just never thought about it. I guess I figured that we all have experiences that make us who we are, and I had mine just like everyone else. It wasn't until recently, as I started to share my story with others, that I started to realize I had come into this world in the midst of what most would consider unusual circumstances. Some of those circumstances wouldn't be made clear to me for over a quarter century. Some spanned generations. I, however, had no idea how unusual any of the situations surrounding my birth, childhood, or my family were until well into adulthood.

I was born near Saint Tropez, France in the winter of 1976 to a mother descended from British nobility, and a father who was a celebrated Michelin-starred French chef. My father had graduated from Cordon Bleu, worked as a chef at Chez Maxim in Paris, and served as a parachutist in the French Army before marrying my mother and opening popular restaurants in Vancouver, Canada and on the French Riviera. Although he was a brilliant restauranteur, he was also an alcoholic who swung between being generous and wonderful and emotionally and verbally abusive.

After nine years of that emotional pendulum, my mom had had enough. She sent me with a friend of hers, who looked quite a bit like her, to the resort village of Sainte-Maxime to buy airline tickets to Vancouver. I was only two years old, but I remember being at the travel agency with her friend and hearing her say, "I need tickets for me and my son." I started to say, "You're not my mom," but she hushed me, saying, "I'll explain later." Little did I know that while she was buying our tickets, my mom was gathering a few things from our home and preparing to whisk me away to Canada, where she knew she had a better chance of getting custody of me when she filed for divorce than she would in France.

It didn't take long for my dad to follow us to Vancouver. More than once when he came by our house, my mom, who had gotten a restraining order, had him arrested. After that, he resorted to drunk-dialing our house in the middle of the night while I was in bed. The phone was in the kitchen, which shared a thin wall with my bedroom, and I could hear every word of their conversations as my mom recorded them. Some nights she had to deal with the sad, self-pitying drunk who threatened to kill himself if he didn't get to see me. Other nights he was the raging drunk who threatened to kill my mom and her whole family and take me back to France. I had nightmares about being killed at my grandmother's house. When we were out after dark, I worried he might be lurking behind a tree with a knife. I was terrified of my father, but I also longed to have a relationship with him, and for our lives to go back to normal.

I was a bright child. I walked and talked early. I had a mind that questioned the way things worked—the whys behind the whats. I loved to take things apart and put things together with my hands and with my mind. Though I was analytical, as a child I also had a great faith in the miraculous. I believed in God and guardian angels, the tooth fairy, the Easter bunny, and Santa Claus. When I went in the woods, I thought I might see a gnome, or find a leprechaun's gold if I could just find the spot where the rainbow ended. I was filled with wonder, and expected the wonderful to happen.

When I was four years old, a friend from day care invited me to Sunday School. I ended up going every week for two years, even though my friend never returned after the first week. For two hours each Sunday, I experienced peace and sang songs about Jesus, who loved me, and who I immediately added to the pantheon of miraculous beings in whom I believed.

Of all these beings, however, the one I worshiped most was Santa. I believed that he was watching me, knew all about me, and cared if I was naughty or nice. Every December, my number-one priority was to get to the mall, sit on his lap, and petition him to bring me what I wanted for Christmas. I remember worrying that if I didn't get a chance to tell him, I wouldn't get what I wanted.

My belief in and love for Santa filled me with wonder. I knew all the songs about him, both in English and French. I loved Christmas songs because they filled me with hope for what I knew was coming. My favorite Christmas song was "Petit Garçon" by Nana Mouskouri:

Dans son manteau rouge et blanc
Sur un traineau porté par le vent
Il descendra par la cheminée
Petit garçon, il est l'heure d'aller se coucher
Tes yeux se voilent
Ecoute les étoiles
Tout est calme, reposé
Entends-tu les clochettes tintinnabuler?
Et demain matin petit garçon
Tu trouveras dans tes chaussons
Tous les jouets dont tu as révais
Petit garçon il est l'heure d'aller se coucher

Or, roughly translated:

In his coat of red and white
On a sled carried by the wind
He will go down the chimney
Little boy, it's time to go to bed
Your eyes veil themselves
Listen to the stars
Everything is calm, rested
Do you hear the tinkle tinkle of the bells?
And tomorrow morning, little boy
You will find in your slippers
All the toys you've dreamed of
Little boy, it's time to go to bed

As Christmas drew near, I dreamed more and more about this wonderful day when Santa would come. I was completely enamored with the idea that there was a nice man who loved children, who longed for us to be good people, and who spent his year building toys to show us how much he loved us.

For me, Christmas wasn't just about the presents, but about the wonder, goodness, and joy of the season. On Christmas, my mom threw the rules out the window and let me see my dad unsupervised. It was a day where only good was allowed, when I believed nothing bad could happen. This was why it was by far my favorite holiday.

The Christmas just before my fifth birthday, I woke up early to see what was under the tree. My mom and her boyfriend were still in bed, but she had said I could open one present before they got up. That year the biggest present was from my dad—the box was bigger than me! I ripped off the wrapping paper and saw the picture on the box. A Pianosaurus! It was exactly what it sounds like—a dinosaur with a piano built into its back—and it was the most popular toy everyone wanted that year. I couldn't believe it. I hadn't even dared to ask Santa for a present that good. My dad was the best. Yes, sometimes he terrified me, but it was Christmas, the one perfect day of the year. He had just given me the best present ever, he loved me, and everything was good in the world.

The Pianosaurus came with color-coded sheet music and corresponding color-coded keys. I learned five songs perfectly before my mom and her boyfriend even got out of bed. I begged my mom to let me take the Pianosaurus with us when we went over to see my dad later that morning. She thought it was too big, but at last I convinced her. I couldn't wait to show my dad the songs I had learned. I knew he was going to be so proud.

Sure enough, when I played for him, he was blown away. He said I was a prodigy, and that one day he would buy me a Steinway concert grand. I remember every detail of that day. He was a world-class chef and offered to make me anything I wanted for lunch. I wanted French fries, so he made them for me. We laughed and played. When my mom came to get me, I didn't want to go, and I didn't want to leave my Pianosaurus, which she said I should do. It had started raining (as it often does in Vancouver) and she said it would get ruined by the rain. I really wanted to bring it home, but it was my favorite toy and I didn't want to ruin it, so I left it at my dad's. She promised I could see him again the next day and pick it up

That night, I was awakened by the sounds of my mom and dad fighting on the phone. Immediately, I knew I wasn't going to see my dad the next day. I was crushed. As it turned out, it was over a week before I was able to see him again. Every day, I begged my mom to take me there to get my Pianosaurus. Finally, we arranged to go over to my dad's. I couldn't wait to play the Pianosaurus. I literally ran from the car all the way to his apartment. When I got there, however, it was gone. My dad said that he had lent it to his friend's daughter, who had come over while I'd been away. I begged and begged him to get it back so I could take it home. That toy was almost all I had thought about since the last time I'd seen him. My mom stepped in to the conversation with my dad, which escalated into a fight in which the truth came out that he had gotten drunk and given the Pianosaurus away to his friend's daughter. I was devastated. I couldn't understand why my own father would give away something that I loved so much. It didn't make any sense to me. Why would he care more about some little girl he hardly knew than his own son?

I didn't see my dad for a while after that. He could only see me with a court-appointed supervisor as a condition of the divorce, and I think he didn't like the idea of someone being in control over how and when he could see his son, so he just opted out.

At Sunday school, I found some comfort learning about God, who they said was a "perfect father." I didn't know what that meant, exactly, but the church people were really nice, so I went, and sang the songs, and colored pictures of Jonah and the whale. I went every week by myself for two years—until the day I lost hope in the miraculous.

I was walking to the bus after kindergarten one day when a first-grader pulled me aside and said, "Hey kid, guess what? Santa's not real!"

"What are you talking about?" I retorted. "Of course he's real."

"No, he's not," he insisted. "Tonight when you get home, ask your mom."

I knew he was serious. You never ask an adult if you're not 100% sure of yourself. So I stayed and asked him what he knew. As a result, I missed the bus, and my mom had to leave work to come pick me up. It didn't take her long on the ride home to discern that I was upset.

"Are you okay?" she asked.

"Yeah."

"Did something happen?"

"No."

"Did someone do something to you?"

"No."

"Do you want to talk about it?"

"There's nothing to talk about."

When we got home, she sat me down on our stoop, looked me dead in the eye and said, "Please tell me what's wrong. I promise I won't be mad."

It took me a few minutes to ask the question to which no kid wants an answer. "Is Santa Claus real?"

She paused.

And I knew.

She fumbled with a weak excuse. "Oh, sweetie . . . we're all Santa's helpers."

But I knew. So, I said, "The tooth fairy, the Easter bunny, and God—they're not real either, are they?"

There was no answering that. I had thrown every supernatural being adults had told me about into the same bucket, and that bucket had been emptied in one fell swoop. Everything I had believed in, hoped in, was gone. My mom tried to comfort me, but it was useless. I didn't understand why she would lie—and why adults everywhere would conspire in that lie. Why would she let me believe the tooth fairy brought me money, and the Easter bunny brought me candy, and Jesus loved me? Why would she want me to believe that Santa brought me the best presents? Why would she let me believe a fictitious man loved me more than she did? If Santa wasn't real, who was going to know or care if I was naughty or nice?

Something in me changed that day. I didn't dream the same after that. I didn't trust the same after that, and I certainly didn't believe the same after that, either. I started stealing and lying. I knew it was wrong, but I didn't care. I stole caramels from the corner store almost every day, and toys from the drug store. Sometimes I got caught and punished, but it didn't stop me from stealing. I honestly don't know why I did it—if it was rebellion or if I just liked the rush. But if God didn't exist and Santa wasn't real, what was the point in not doing it?

Everything had changed—the way I saw the world, and my place in it. Now my destiny was my own to make, and along with my fresh disregard for the rules, I developed a new drive to make my own rules and be the best at whatever I was doing. The first year I played soccer, our team dominated the league. The next year, when I was six, the coaches thought I showed leadership potential, so they made me the captain of a team with a bunch of new kids who didn't know how to play. I didn't see it as an opportunity to raise them up, however. I only saw them as holding me back. If we couldn't be the best, I didn't want to participate. The first time we played my old team, I tore off my jersey and started scoring goals against my own team. The coaches pulled me out and said I couldn't do that. I told them I didn't want to be team captain of a team that sucked—I wanted to be on my old team. They said it didn't work that way, so I quit the league.

When I was seven, my mom and I moved from Vancouver to San Diego. When we were packing boxes, I found two Playboy magazines in my mom's old boyfriend's nightstand. I had never seen magazines full of nude women before, and asked my mom what they were. She was studying psychology and didn't want me to think sex was something to be ashamed of or couldn't be talked about openly, so she said I could have them.

I didn't know what people did with those kind of magazines, but I was old enough to know that other kids didn't have them. When I moved to San Diego, I showed them to other kids so they'd think I was cool. Some older kids thought I had the coolest mom on the planet, while other kids weren't allowed to come over to my house. When I discovered more porn magazines stashed in forts kids had built in the rural areas near our house, I stole them and added them to my growing collection.

The week after we moved in, I was drawing on a sketchpad in my front yard when two girls I recognized from school rode up on their bikes. One of the girls got off her pink Huffy with a hot-pink banana seat and streamers on the handlebars. She walked up to me and said, "Hi, I'm

Laurie. I live down the street. I think I saw you at school. Did you just move in?"

"Yeah, I'm Morgan. We just moved in last week."
"What are you drawing?"
"I don't know yet. I'm still thinking about it."
"Oh, well, can I see your sketchpad?"
"There's nothing in it. I usually take my drawings out and put them up or in my drawer when I'm done."
"Oh. Um . . . can I still see your sketchpad, though?"

I thought I was making a friend, so I handed the sketchpad to her. Instead of looking at it, she ran to her bike. She and her friend laughed at me as they rode away.

Furious, I ran after her, screaming obscenities. She rode to the end of a cul-de-sac a few blocks away. I chased her all the way there, yelling at her as I ran. Our neighborhood was full of kids and they all came out to see what was going on.

When I reached Laurie, she was dangling my sketchpad over a storm drain, threatening to toss it in. It seemed like all the other kids were joining in, teasing me. I was begging her to give it back, choking back tears. Without a word, she dropped the sketchpad into the drain.

I knew I wasn't supposed to hit a girl, but I wanted to attack her. I happened to have a pair of heavy steel kitchen shears in my pocket—I had all my art supplies out on the front lawn when Laurie showed up—and I pulled them out and threw them at her. As they flew out of my hand, they opened like a throwing star and stuck in her head right between her eyes. Kids started screaming. Laurie stood there in shock as dark blood ran down her face.

I turned and ran all the way home. As I ran through the front door, I screamed, "I stabbed Laurie!" My mom found me hiding under my bed, crying, and asked me what happened and where Laurie was. After I told her, she hurried to the cul-de-sac, found Laurie, and took her to the hospital.

My mom and Laurie's parents got together and decided the best punishment was to force us to become friends. I was a latchkey kid, because my mom was in school. Laurie's mom volunteered to watch me after school so I could do homework with Laurie and play with her older brother and some of the other neighborhood kids with some supervision.

One afternoon, Laurie's mom went to the store and left us alone at their house. Laurie's brother had football practice, so it was just the two of us watching Mickey's Mousercise on the Disney Channel. Laurie turned to me and asked, "Do you want to play the humping game?"

I had never heard of that game before, so I asked her what it was. She ran upstairs and brought down a video tape. "Here, I'll show you."

I'd never seen a porn movie before, and had no idea what the adults were doing.

"They're humping," Laurie said. "That's the humping game."

I knew that what we were about to do was wrong, but I also was intrigued. I knew it was something grownups did, and I wanted to feel grown up. I was seven years old, and Laurie was eight and a half. I did my best to imitate what I had just watched, but I couldn't shake the feeling that it was wrong.

Over the course of the next two years, Laurie and I played that game multiple times. Sometimes it just the two of us, and sometimes she got other girls and boys from the neighborhood involved. Pleasure mixed with shame, and the rush of doing something bad, left me confused. Part of me hated the shame I felt, but part of me loved the thrill of the forbidden and the fear of getting caught.

Then one day we were all watching TV in Laurie's living room and someone's four-year-old little brother came over. Laurie forced him to pull down his pants. I tried to stop her, but Laurie yelled at me, so I walked out. As I was leaving, the little boy ran out of the house behind me crying with his pants halfway down. Up until that point, I knew we were doing something bad, but everyone had been a willing participant. This was different—much different. She had done something to that little boy that he didn't want done to him, and I knew that was wrong. I stopped hanging out over at Laurie's house. Around that time, my mom got engaged and we moved to La Jolla, just north of San Diego. I never saw or talked to Laurie again.

☙

La Jolla is one of the most beautiful beach communities in the world. We lived in a mid-century modern house about fifty feet from the ocean. I was in heaven. I had the ocean, a great new group of friends, an awesome new dad, and a new start.

La Jolla also boasts the largest concentration of Nobel laureates in the world. Many of my new friends' parents were successful entrepreneurs, honored scientists, well-known doctors, and lawyers. Though part of me felt that my family's success didn't compare to theirs, another part of me thought, as I sat sharing a meal and conversation with the inventor of the ATM machine, a Nobel-prize winning scientist, the founder of an iconic American brand, or a multi-Oscar-winning composer, that all of these people were just people, and anything was possible. Other times, I doubted myself and saw where I fell short. But I could hold my own in conversation with these great men and women, and I dreamt of the possibility that lay ahead of me.

I loved science, art, business and design. I had tested with an IQ score of 164 at the age of seven. I was also a good arguer with high stamina, and if I wanted to be right, I'd just keep talking until my opponent gave up. Sometimes this worked to my advantage, sometimes it didn't.

One night, I was at a friend's house and invited to stay for dinner. Lalo Schifrin, the legendary composer who wrote Theme to Mission Impossible, among other iconic compositions, was the guest of honor. He and

I started a conversation, but instead of listening to the stories of his incredible life, I felt the need to compete with him, almost as if I needed to prove myself to this great man. I remember thinking, Shut up, Morgan. What are you doing? It was the first of many situations I can remember where I should have been honored to just be listening, but instead felt I needed to be recognized as worthy and have an answer for everything. However, I realized there were some questions that I couldn't answer.

Why was I full of fear? Why, in a room filled with people who loved me, did that love not feel like it was enough? Why did I stay up at night in bed worrying about things I couldn't quite put my finger on, feeling like the other shoe was always about to drop? Why were people whom I judged as less intelligent and talented than me experiencing success and happiness, while I never was quite able to get there?

CHAPTER 2:
Illegitimate Solutions to Legitimate Problems

I longed for a real connection with friends. I remember seeing the movie Stand By Me, and thinking, That's how friendship is supposed to look. My group of friends actually looked a lot like that group of friends in the movie, and we did similar things . . . I, however, always felt like the odd man out. Even when I was in a crowd of people who claimed to love me, I didn't feel it. I didn't feel like I fit in. I always felt like I needed to compete, and I frequently felt like no matter what I said or did, I was always misunderstood.

My friends and I discovered alcohol and drugs the summer after sixth grade. I was twelve. I smoked pot before I drank, because alcohol terrified me.

One night, a friend drank a fifth of tequila and came over to a mutual friend's house. He proceeded to tell us his deepest, darkest secrets about abuse he suffered as a child, horrifically embarrassing moments in his life, lies he'd told, and crippling self-doubt he carried. He cried, hugged us, told us how much he loved us, said we were his only true friends . . . and then he ran to the bathroom and threw up.

I felt like throwing up, I was so embarrassed for the guy. I honestly had never felt as awkward in my life as I did in that moment. My other friend turned to me and said, "Well, that's one thing about booze—it'll make you honest."

I was already worried about following in my father's footsteps and becoming an alcoholic, but that experience sealed it. If I let my friends know how little I thought of myself, confessed all my fears and self-doubt, it would be over. So, I smoked pot and started to dabble in other drugs, but swore I'd never drink.

That lasted about six months.

One night at a party, my most uptight, neurotic friend drank, and he came alive. He went from quiet and reserved to being the life of the party—no tears, nothing weird, just fearless and alive! I thought, Maybe it's not that bad . . . I got drunk that night and loved it. I felt uninhibited and like I finally belonged with this group of friends, among whom I had secretly felt unworthy. I felt invincible, and I didn't ever want that feeling to leave. From then on, I tried to stay as drunk or high as possible for as long as possible.

During this time, as with most boys going through puberty, sex also became a huge focus in my life. I discovered masturbation and finally figured out what pornography was really used for. Among my friends, porn became a major commodity and sex the main topic of conversation. We traded magazines and videos with each other and talked about losing our virginity like it was a race to the finish line. However, I didn't dare tell them about the sexual experiences I had already had.

I had a best friend with whom I shared almost everything. Nearly every weekend, we spent the night at each other's houses and stayed up late into the night in conversation, often discussing the girls at school we fantasized about. One night, one of us had gotten a hold of a porn movie and we watched it together in his room. About ten minutes in, he offered me some lotion to masturbate with. It was super awkward, but I took the cue. A few minutes later, he suggested we masturbate each other. I went along with it. Then he offered to give me a blow job. At first I turned him down. I was already feeling uncomfortable and ashamed. But there was pleasure mixed with that shame, and I didn't want it to stop. He offered again, and this time I said, "Okay." I climaxed almost immediately. I couldn't believe what I had just done. He tried to get me to finish him off but I couldn't even look at him.

The next morning, I made some excuse about needing to write a report that I forgot was due Monday, and had my mom pick me up early. I don't know if my friend knew I was lying, but I had to get away from him, I was so ashamed.

The shame didn't keep me away for long, though. A few weeks later, I stayed over again. The same thing happened, and again, pleasure was mixed with shame. Over the course of the next two years, we experimented with each other almost every time I spent the night. He kept trying to push things further, urging me to have sex with him, but I refused. That was too much. I finally started making excuses not to go over to his house.

Meanwhile, I joined another group of friends who had a band, and became their singer. My life started to center around music, drugs, and parties. I had a great voice, but struggled with crippling stage fright, and could only really perform if I was wasted. I believed I had it in me to be great, and when I was drunk I felt like I could take on the world. But when I was sober, the shame I was carrying kept me from looking people in the eye.

Eventually, I stopped singing and started managing a band as well as booking and promoting shows at an all-ages venue. I began hanging out with older musicians and was out almost every night. By this time, I was a sophomore in high school and the popular seniors at school started coming to me for help getting bands for their parties. Before long, I was being invited everywhere, it seemed. I'd found a niche and become somewhat popular. Yet though I outwardly posed as a cool kid, inwardly I still had intense self-doubt. As long as I was loaded, I felt like I was on top of the world, but when I wasn't, my fear and self-loathing became excruciating. Lots of things happened when I was loaded that I never intended. I said and did a lot things I was ashamed of. There were also things I did to others and things that were done to me that I barely remembered or didn't remember at all.

One night, I ran into a girl I had known since fourth grade at the club I booked shows for. She couldn't believe I worked for this club—to her it was the coolest thing in the world. After the show, we met up to drink and get high. Without even having a conversation about it, I found myself back at her house having sex. Just like every other casual sexual encounter I had had in my life, shame quickly followed, along with fear that this girl was going to think that because we had sex, we were now boyfriend and girlfriend. In my neighborhood, or at least amongst my friends, that was the way relationships worked—you met a girl, had sex with her, and then she was your girlfriend. In all honesty, this girl wasn't ugly, but she also wasn't one of the "hot" girls at school and wouldn't impress my friends. I couldn't bring myself to talk to her directly, so I spoke to her best friend, who was dating a friend of mine, to make sure the girl understood that we weren't together. It bothered me that I was so shallow—she gave her virginity to me and all I could think of was my reputation—but I was. Again, I felt pleasure and shame, but of a different kind.

In the end, I undermined my reputation all on my own. I started stealing from family and friends to stay loaded, and very quickly found that I was no longer welcome at houses and parties where I had been the guest of honor. My parents started locking their bedroom door when they weren't home. I resented them for not trusting me, started fighting with them a lot, and stopped coming home—at first for days, then weeks. I tried to stay at friends' houses where I knew they would be too polite to tell me to leave, but some nights, I couldn't find a place to stay, so I slept on the beach. I probably slept at least twenty days on the beach the summer before my junior year.

I knew that was not the way it was supposed to be for a smart, sixteen-year-old kid from a good family, but I was convinced it was everyone else's fault but mine. I decided schools weren't built for kids like me. I was too smart and got bored too easily. I needed someone who recognized my unique giftedness and could pander to that. Or maybe my parents didn't love me enough, or too much, or not in the right way. I believed if I could only get people to do what I wanted, the world would be a better place, for me and for them. Trouble was, whenever I got what I wanted, I realized that it wasn't what I wanted, or didn't do for me what I thought it would. Still, I held on to the idea that there was an elusive "something" that would make my life better, and everyone else just needed to change for me to find it.

I didn't think I had a drug and alcohol problem. I was aware that other people had a problem with the way I drank and used drugs, but it was their problem, not mine. When I was loaded, I was fine. The only time I felt ashamed was when I ran into friends who were achieving real success in school, getting good grades and in to good colleges, and excelling in sports. Though I kept up a good front and focused on all the "cool" stuff that I was doing, deep down I felt like I was made for more, but just couldn't get there. So, I kept using drugs and alcohol to run from my shame, disappointment, and sense of powerlessness. Like all addicts (though I didn't believe I was one), I was using drugs as an illegitimate solution to a very real problem..

☙

One night, after selling the last of my CDs and stealing and selling a pair of jeans to scrape enough money together to get high, then finding I didn't have enough drugs or alcohol to get to oblivion, I ran into an old friend named Erik. Erik had been fun to get high with—until he had gotten sober about six months earlier and disappeared from our group of friends. I started in on him, telling him what a mess things were, blaming all my problems on anyone I could think of.

Erik was usually a good, non-judgmental listener. He also had a job and a truck, and I thought I might get him to buy me food—I was starving after spending all my money to get high. This night was different, though. He listened to me whine for a minute or two, then cut me off.

"You know you don't have to live like this if you don't want to," he said.

"What do you mean?" I asked. "What do you think I should do? Go to AA?"

He looked at me, raised an eyebrow, and smiled.

"Seriously? What do you do for fun? It seems like you go to meetings, listen to people talk about themselves, drink coffee, listen to people talk about themselves some more, and maybe on a really good night you get to go bowling! That sounds like hell."

Still looking me straight in the eye he said, "It's not like that. Well, actually . . . It's kind of like that. But it's not all like that. You know me—if it totally sucked, do you think I'd stay?"

I couldn't disagree with that point.

"Sobriety gives me a life," he continued. "When I was getting high, that's all I could do. My relationships sucked, I hated myself, and I couldn't even show up for my kid brother."

That sounded like me.

"But only six months sober, I have great relationships," he continued. "I look forward to getting up. I have a great job, a great girlfriend, and I get to be a good big brother. My dad even just co-signed a loan so I could get a truck."

I didn't have any of that. I had robbed my little brother's piggy bank to get high just a few weeks before.

The Power to Change

I decided to give sobriety a try. I was pretty sure I wasn't really a drug addict or alcoholic, and that circumstances were my problem. On the other hand, circumstances had brought me Eric when I had run out of friends, so I was willing to give it a go.

I went home and told my parents that I needed to do home study for my junior year because I had a problem using drugs every day at school, and they supported my decision. I started going to AA meetings every night and began making friends with people I met there, most of whom were ten to twenty years older than I was. I still doubted whether I really belonged there—whether alcohol was really my problem—but I liked the changes that came with getting sober. I had the freedom and time to get a full-time job and make money. I finally started working out and getting in shape. Over that year, I went from being the guy nobody had wanted to be around to being envied by my old friends.

The only problem was that I traded drugs and alcohol for all these good pursuits without dealing with the things inside me—the restlessness, fear, self-doubt, and misery that for me, could only be fixed with a drink or a drug. I was able to distract myself from them during the day by staying busy, but at night they kept me awake like a pulsing, raw nerve. I had night terrors where I felt like some force was holding me down in my bed—sometimes it got so bad, I felt I couldn't breathe.

Soon, the novelty of sobriety, the excitement about freedom and money, and the pleasure of feeling like a grown-up faded, and my view of recovery grew cynical. After being sober for more than a year, I had an apartment steps from the ocean, a job that I loved, friends, and a relationship with my family again, but none of it brought me peace. All the things that had once felt like freedom now began to feel like a giant burden others were putting on me—my friends expected too much of me, my job asked too much of me, AA people were crazy, and it seemed my brother had it way easier than I did at his age.

The Power to Change

I started hanging out with my old friends. When I had left them behind to get sober, I had by far been the biggest mess among them. Now I discovered that these occasional drinkers and daily pot-smokers had graduated to intravenous heroin use. I began watching them get high. After they shot up and jerked loose the belt tied around their bicep, I'd see the rush come over them. It looked like relief. I hadn't experienced relief in ages, and I longed for it.

I kept going to AA meetings, however, half terrified of going back to my old life and half wanting to keep my new life as Mr. Young Joe Sober. But at the meetings I started complaining. I explained that I was caught between two worlds—no one besides my junkie friends understood me, and AA was robbing me of my youth. I took pride in my now two years of sobriety, but continued to spend time with my friends, who were beginning to use heroin and cocaine daily. I even started buying drugs, toying with the idea of getting high, then selling them back later the same night, cursing myself for a coward.

I started fixating on the idea that I didn't belong in AA—that I had come under false pretenses. I had asked a guy I envied for being popular and put-together) to be my sponsor (AA mentor), but never truly opened up to him as he guided me through the 12 Steps, and blamed the process for not working for me. AA's 12 Steps are like Christian repentance unpacked into digestible chunks. Steps 4 and 5 deal with confession—inner, then outer. In Step 4, you take an inventory of unforgiveness, fear, and sexual misconduct, and in Step 5, you confess that inventory out loud to yourself, God, and the sponsor. Steps 6 and 7 deal with heart-change through contrition, or broken-heartedness. After recognizing the reality of the brokenness that comes from trying to live life to the best of your ability without God, in Step 7 you pray to God to remove every defect of character that stand in the way of usefulness to God and man. That leads into Steps 8 and 9, which involve making amends to those you used to hate, and those you have harmed. Obviously, each of these steps relies on belief and power from God. But I had lost my faith years earlier. I tried to comfort myself by intellectualizing spirituality, and I could speak eloquently on spiritual topics, but my insomnia and my anxiety were getting much worse, as was my resentment against AA and its members.

I started contemplating suicide and testing God. One Friday night after getting paid, I took my entire check and bought a gram of heroin and two grams of cocaine—enough drugs to kill an elephant several times over. I was going to kill myself by shooting the world's biggest speedball. I said to God, "If You're real, You won't let me die," but thought, If He's not, at least I'll die with a smile on my face. (In reality, that much cocaine would be an awful and terrifying way to die, but I wasn't thinking that at the time.)

I headed to the motorhome behind my friend Sam's house to watch my friends get high before shooting the speedball. Nobody knew what I was about to do. I didn't really want to die, but I also didn't really want to live. I felt like an outsider looking in on my own life—an observer, not a participant. I knew that there was something buried deep inside of me, a great potential for something, but it seemed I was the butt of some cosmic joke and would never quite reach it no matter how hard I tried. I sat on the floor in that motorhome, scraping the cocaine from side to side on a CD case with a razor blade as I contemplated death and silently prayed that God, who I didn't believe in, would give me a sign.

Then my friend Sam, who had just shot up, looked down at me and said in a nasal, junkie murmur, "I don't know if you're thinking about getting high, but when you used to get high, you were an annoying f**k. I like having you around sober. If you get high, don't expect me to want to hang out."

Active drug addicts don't tell their friends not to use drugs, especially when they are high. That never happens. Misery loves company. Was this my sign from God? I snapped back to my senses. What was I thinking? I wanted to live! That was all the sign I needed. I left the drugs there and walked away. I never went back to that house or to those friends—I was too terrified.

I told my AA sponsor what had happened, redoubled my efforts at the 12 Steps, and let the fear kept me sober for a while. I started going to college and getting straight As, and soon discovered something I was passionate about and wanted to study—graphic design. A trendy boutique advertising agency in San Diego offered me my first professional job as a junior designer. I got a title and my first business card, and started working on cool projects and making real money...

*

During spring break of 1995, some friends from high school visited me at college. I wasn't planning on drinking, but I wanted to impress them, especially the girls, by buying alcohol for everyone. I was nineteen, but I had a fake ID and money. I spent almost $300 on liquor for five non-alcoholics and a Coke and some chips for myself. Then one of the girls asked me to crack open a bottle of Southern Comfort for her. As I passed it to her, I smelled it, and it smelled like freedom. She took one swig, spit it out, and handed the bottle back to me without a top. I walked away from the group with the bottle and sat by myself looking up at the stars. I prayed again to a God I claimed I didn't believe in to give me a sign, but nothing came.

I had gotten to the point where I truly didn't believe I had a drinking problem. I had forgotten how much I used to drink and how I lost control when I did. Even though I had faithfully attended AA for two and a half years, no one had successfully convinced me that I had an addiction or explained how unlikely it was that I would be able to stop drinking or using if I opened that door again. Not every addict goes off the rails every time they drink or use, but they can't predict if or when they will. As an analogy, if I had a car with brakes that worked ninety percent of the time, would it be safe to drive the car? Definitely not. I brake more than ten times every time I drive. I'd have a one-in-ten chance of totaling my car and injuring others and myself every time I stepped on the brake. It would never be a sane choice to drive that car, even if it was a one-in-hundred chance. Alcoholism and addiction are like that—alcoholics can't stay stopped on their own. In the years that I drank heavily, I could and did stop for days or weeks, but I couldn't stay that way. I had dozens of times where my heart was beating out of my chest and I thought I was going to die, or the room was spinning, or we were about to be arrested, and I prayed to God to make it stop and promised I would never do this again. If someone had hooked me up to a lie detector and asked if I made that promise sincerely, I would have passed with flying colors, because I meant it. But no matter how sincere I was or wanted to be, within a matter of days or weeks, I was at it again.

None of that past behavior seemed that bad as I sat there, clutching a liter of SoCo 110, waiting for a sign from God to get me to not drink. All I knew was that I felt like I didn't fit anywhere in the world—not in AA, not with my peers. I thought, I can't go back to my meetings not knowing for sure whether I belong. I walked back towards the group, hearing the laughter and conversation that was flowing more freely because my friends were drinking. About fifteen feet away, I couldn't take it anymore. I stopped, put the bottle to my lips, and took a huge swig. It burned going down, and as I felt it hit my stomach, I thought, Oh my God. I relapsed.

Now that it was official, I figured I might as well drink the whole bottle. I stood there and drank three-fourths of that bottle in about five minutes, stopping to choke it back down when I started to gag. As I felt the familiar fog of drunkenness start to settle in, I walked up to my friends and asked if anyone knew where I could score some cocaine, because I was about to be really, really drunk.

My friend Ross said, "Drunk? You don't even drink!"

I breathed in his face.

"Holy s**t!" he exclaimed. "Welcome back! Hey, Morgan's drunk! Woohoo!" He had forgotten, just as I had, the reality of my past drinking life.

I woke up on a sober friend's couch the following morning very hung over. Apparently, I had called in the middle of the night, remorseful and asking to be picked up. They had come, taken me to get some food in my stomach, and gotten me to bed. First thing in the morning, they took me to an AA meeting, which was terrible. "A head full of AA and a belly full of booze," they urged, "is a bad combination." I thought, It was one bad night. What did you expect? Of course my first night drinking in two and a half years was going to be bad. I just have to figure out how to drink normally.

But in truth, I never wanted to drink normally. One glass of wine with a nice dinner, leaving a little at the bottom of the glass? No, thank you. Who was I kidding? I wanted to drink heavily, manage my drinking with a cocaine habit, and not experience any consequences. I wanted oblivion without the hangovers or the judgment of others, because that's the only time I could recall when my skin felt like it fit right, when I felt connected to life, and when I felt like I could love others and accept their love in return.

I tried to achieve that. I failed. I tried again. I failed. And failed and failed and failed.

In less than two weeks, my life was spiraling downward. I was fired from my ad agency job for attacking my boss while drunk at a bar. I had been in an upper division design class that met at 8 a.m. on Tuesday and Thursday and had a two-absence automatic failure policy. I missed a Tuesday class after staying up all night drinking vodka and smoking cocaine, and I knew I was going to miss Thursday morning, so I got on the university phone system and withdrew from all my classes.

I was fully aware that losing the best job I had ever had and becoming a college dropout were both results of drinking again, yet still insisted to myself that my inability to drink successfully was the result of a neurosis that I had picked up being sober in AA for over two years. In my mind, I had been a model AA member. I had done the 12 Steps, gone to loads of meetings, and always had a service commitment. It's easy to avoid dealing with your own issues while you're busy doing "work" for others that legitimately needs to get done. Not only is it easy to hide out in service—people tend to encourage you in it. I did a lot of that. I was busy. I went to school full-time, worked full-time, went to around eight AA meetings a week, had service commitments at six of them, had a girlfriend, and worked out five days a week. I barely had time to think. Most nights I was so exhausted I would collapse into bed. The nights where I wasn't thoroughly exhausted, I lay awake in bed obsessing about things in my life I had no control over. I was filled with fear, waiting for the other shoe to drop. And the Steps I had claimed to have done? I hadn't really made amends to anyone. I didn't need God. I didn't practice prayer or meditation. As for the searching and fearless moral inventory I had supposedly done—I had made stuff up and left stuff off, trying to impress a sponsor I respected but couldn't open up to.

I've heard it said that addicts and alcoholics are in denial. I don't believe that. Denial is knowing the truth but denying it to avoid feeling uncomfortable. Delusion is actually believing something is true that is not. That was me, and I was very vocal in my beliefs. I was boldly delusional. My life was falling apart, but for every new failure, I had a new excuse that I actually believed.

Somehow, I managed to get my old job back at Starbucks. I had been a superstar when I worked there before, outselling all my retail partners and winning more Bravos (Starbucks' recognition program for outstanding service) than anyone else in the store. My former manager rehired me, expecting to have the same confident, intelligent, sober Morgan back on her team. Instead, in just six weeks, I was written up five times for things that should have resulted in me being immediately fired. Twice, I showed up for a five-a.m. shift after staying up all night binging on cocaine and vodka, still so drunk I was incapable of opening the store. I got caught stashing liquor in the employee bathroom to nurse a bad hangover. While not on shift, I showed up belligerently drunk with a group of friends and insisted on going behind the counter to make my friends drinks. I was found passed out behind the store. Yet for some reason, my manager believed in me so much that she gave me second chance after second chance.

My self-destructive streak finally came to a crash-point one Friday night. I got drunk, smoked cocaine, and went to an end-of-year concert at my college. I was such a mess I couldn't even stand up. I ended up getting in an altercation with a friend of my girlfriend, after which my girlfriend decided she had finally had enough and dumped me. After that, I broke into a friend's dorm room to smoke pot. I have a hazy memory of not being able to find him, being hassled by security guards for being too drunk, losing my wallet, and finally walking miles to my friend's parents' house in the middle of the night. I let myself in through the back door and passed out.

The next morning, I woke up and tried to piece together the spotty memories from the night before. Then I remembered I had to be at work at Starbucks in an hour—I couldn't be even one minute late. My boss had made it clear that, though she loved me, if I did anything else wrong, I was done.

I showed up on time that Saturday morning and tried to fix my oncoming hangover with coffee, orange juice, and lots of water. It didn't work. Instead, I ended up having a panic attack while stationed at the espresso machine. My manager tried to help by sending me to brew coffee instead, but I ended up shaking so badly that I dropped the pot and drenched myself in scalding coffee.

When my manager found me in the employee breakroom, she immediately demanded, "What's wrong with you?"

I began rattling off excuses. "My girlfriend and I broke up. I lost my friends at a concert and had to walk home. I'm sorry I'm a little on edge. I had a rough night."

"Rough night? It's been a rough month. Every day it's another excuse. What happened to the Morgan who used to work here—the one that was my superstar? The award winner? What happened to those meetings you used to go to?"

"I don't think I'm really an alcoholic," I explained. "I used to go to those meetings because I thought I was, but then I realized that it was those meetings that were making me crazy. I'm just trying to figure out how to drink normally." Even as I said those words, I was struck with their hollowness.

"Morgan," she replied, "I don't think you'll ever drink normally. I've talked to almost everyone here—or, well, they've talked to me—and they're all worried about you. The group you went to Mexico with for Karla's birthday told me how you almost got everyone arrested. No one wants to work with you, because they don't know who they're going to get—if you're going to be 'here' or in your own little world. I can't do it anymore. I can't keep making excuses for you. You know I've known a lot of people in recovery over the years, and plenty who have relapsed. I've never met one who has been able to relapse successfully, and I don't want to see you die."

"So, I'm fired?" I asked.

"No. I'm going to give you one more chance, but there are some things you're going to have to do. First, I'm taking you off the schedule for eight days. I want you to go back to your meetings every day for those eight days and get a slip signed to show me that you've gone. If you can do that, you still have a job."

I was overwhelmed with more emotions than I could count. I eked out a feeble, "Thank you," and ran into the little employee bathroom to hide my emotions.

Part of me was deeply touched that she cared enough to give me another undeserved chance, but I was also angry. Who was she to tell me to go back to AA? Was it even legal to give me what was effectively a Starbucks court card? Could I do it? Could I go back? Was I really an alcoholic and an addict?

As I went to the bathroom sink to wash the tears off my face, I looked in the mirror and, for the first time in my life, I saw the truth of what I had become. I saw an addict and alcoholic staring back at me. I knew everything in my life needed to change completely. I also knew that I had no power in me to change on my own.

I can't describe the depth of my despair. I felt like walls were closing in on me from all sides, leaving me with nowhere to go. I had known sadness and frustration before, but nothing like this. In a moment of desperation, the only thing that seemed to make sense was to get down on my knees and cry out to a God I didn't know or understand.

I just said three simple words, "God, help me," and the floodgates opened. I ugly-cried on the floor of that bathroom for a good forty-five minutes. Something happened in that time, though. The deluded obsession I had carried for years, that I would somehow be able to control and enjoy my life and the circumstances around me while successfully manage heavy drinking and drug use, which had always led me back to the drug or the bottle, was lifted. My life was still in shambles, but as I snuck out the back door to go to the beach, I felt hope for the first time in what seemed like forever.

As I sat at the beach, I found myself talking to God. Lies that I had told myself for ages began to unravel—blame I had assigned, unforgiveness I had carried, responsibilities I had shirked. It was strange, though—all of these came to light, but not in a way that brought shame. I thought, God I don't know what to do with this mess, and I felt Him reply, "Don't worry, kiddo, I've got you covered."

I went to a meeting that night. It was a meeting I had considered my "home group"—somewhere I knew everyone by name, and they knew me. I was filled with apprehension, fearing judgment and shame as I anticipated introducing myself as one in their first thirty days of sobriety… again. But when I walked into the room, there was no judgment, only warm smiles, hugs, and people saying, "Welcome back. We missed you."

The leader spoke for fifteen minutes and then called on members of the group to share, beginning with me. I started talking about all the mess that I'd made of my life during my relapse—the broken hearts, broken promises, and broken dreams. As I spoke, a guy named Ralph started to laugh. This bothered me, but I didn't let on how bothered I was. I just started speaking louder to drown out his laughter. The louder I spoke, it seemed, the harder he laughed.

Finally, I lost my concentration and paused. In that awkward silence, I had an epiphany. I, who had always suffered from a feeling of terminal uniqueness, had become a very typical and predictable alcoholic, just like everyone else in that room. I, who thought I'd never relate, had actually become the thing I had fought so hard not to become. It was completely ironic, and I got the joke. I started to laugh with Ralph, who apparently had gotten the joke first. Soon, everyone in the room had joined in laughing. I felt like I was home.

I knew I had a lot of work to do. I didn't just wake up one day and think, *Today looks like a great day to screw up my life, hurt everyone I've ever loved, and squander my potential.* No one ever thinks that. What turned into an addiction started off as a solution to a problem—the inner conflict I had had as long as I could remember. Just because I was sober didn't mean that would go away. In fact, it insured that it would rise to the surface like a raw nerve. Getting to the root of that became the work. I was going to have to be honest, and I needed help with that. That help came in the form of a man named Nick Lynch.

The Power to Change

CHAPTER 3: I'm Not the One Who's Going to Change Your Life

About a month sober, I got a call inviting me on a road trip up to San Francisco. It was an opportunity to reconnect with the girlfriend who had left me on the last day of my drinking, and some old friends who were in college up there. I also thought I might be able to see some friends who had moved to the city, including Nick, a guy I knew from AA who had moved there to pursue poetry.

I called Nick on my second evening in San Francisco and got his answering machine. His message said that he was reading his poetry that night at a bookstore in Union Square. I hadn't been to San Francisco since I was a small child and had no idea where anything was, but it turned out that Union Square was just a few blocks from where I was staying. I walked down to the address expecting to find a small, dusty bookstore, maybe something out of the Beat era, with five or six people there to watch Nick. Instead, I found a new bookstore called Borders—a massive, four-story building bustling with activity. Spotting a sign for the poetry open-mic night with a picture of Nick, I followed its directions upstairs to the fourth floor and entered a space packed with about four or five hundred people spilling out over the floor. It was standing room only.

I walked around the rows of bookshelves to try to find a good vantage point. As I approached the rear corner of the floor, I walked down an aisle and found Nick on his knees, praying before he took the stage. The sight moved me. Wanting to give him his space, I turned to walk away, but he saw me.

"Oh my gosh, Morgan!" he exclaimed. "What are you doing here? How did you know?"

"Your answering machine. I called."

"Wow. I knew I had to leave that message on there for someone. It was you! It's so great to see you. Give me a hug. I have to go on right now, but let's connect after."

Amazingly, I found a seat. It turned out that Nick was the main event that night. He started speaking and performing, delivering poetry that was so deeply personal and raw, but so empowered. It was like nothing I'd heard before. It was fearless.

As Nick boldly revealed these deeply personal thoughts, feelings, and revelations through his work, I could feel energy rise in the room. The audience started cheering him on, participating in and connecting to his journey, and somehow having a journey of their own. The atmosphere was electric. People who had been sitting were now on their feet cheering him on. This was more than just a poetry reading. Something was happening inside me. A hope was dawning that maybe one day I could be as free as this man.

As he read the last line of his poem, the room erupted into cheers, whistles, screams, and applause. It was the most powerful standing ovation I had ever witnessed. After it ended, Nick walked past the hundreds of people vying for his attention and waiting to congratulate him, straight over to me.

"Hey, Morgan, I've got to stay here and sell books and tapes and talk to people, but I really want to connect with you," he said. "Are you free tomorrow? Do you want to go to a meeting with me in the morning?"

"Sure, I'd love to," I said enthusiastically. "You were incredible tonight, by the way—so inspiring. I'm staying at California and Van Ness. Where are you? I could come meet you."

"Oh, no way! I'm just around the corner from there at Post and Leavenworth. Why don't I walk up there to meet you? Just come down to the corner at nine."

As I left and walked back to my friend's apartment, I felt so inspired. I didn't know if I had ever felt that way before—if I had, it hadn't been since childhood. It was like someone had turned up the saturation on the entire city—colors, sounds, emotions, and energy were all more alive and intense.

The next morning, I couldn't wait to meet Nick. As I stood on the corner waiting, I spotted him in the distance and watched, increasingly fascinated, as he approached. He was interacting with every person he passed, and as he passed them they were all smiling. Who was this guy? There was something about him that was so powerful—he was brightening the day of everyone he met.

We walked to a meeting in the Marina. As I walked in the room, it felt small, dark, and hopeless, and a slight feeling of dread came over me. I had been to meetings like this before. We called them "dark tunnel meetings" because there was no light at the end of them. I was looking forward to spending time with Nick, but I wasn't looking forward to this meeting. But then, Nick walked in behind me, and the temperature of the room began to change. It was like someone had opened the curtains in a hospital room and let light start pouring in. It wasn't just the temperature, it was the whole atmosphere. People began to smile. I didn't know what was about to happen, but I marveled at the change taking place before my eyes. There was something about Nick.

The meeting got underway. Nick was asked to share. Like the night before, his words were filled with hope and power. People who had been sulking in their seats began to smile and laugh. The room was transformed. The dark tunnel had become a breath of fresh air.

After the meeting, there were lively conversations. A few of Nick's friends were there, and they all were as magnetic as he was. They invited me to another meeting later in the day, and Nick asked if I wanted to join him in running errands around the city until then. How could I refuse? Whatever these people had, it seemed infectious, and I wanted it too.

Over the next five hours, it felt like we covered the entire city. Bookstores, coffee-shops—everywhere we went, people loved Nick. We talked and talked. I don't remember the substance of our conversations, but I remember feeling hope rise in me.

Later, we went to Nick's apartment to meet up with some of his friends who wanted to mediate. As we walked up, they were already in the middle of a heated debate centered around sharing and serving in the recovery fellowship. One side insisted that we should be anonymous when sharing about our lives, being careful to not include the names of others in the fellowship with whom we were spending time. The other side argued that our involvement in each other's lives is much more significant than occasionally seeing each other at meetings—that we have meaningful friendships that are much deeper than the friendships we had when drinking, because they're made purposeful in service to others.

Both sides had plenty of examples to bolster their position and were very direct in how they spoke. The level of honesty made me really uncomfortable, because I had never seen a friendship survive this type of conversation before. After everyone had stated their case, one by one they pulled out little notepads and began scribbling. The scene fell silent apart from the sounds of the city and the feverish scratching of pens. I just sat and watched. Several minutes passed, and the writing stopped. Then, one by one, they started to make amends with each other. Somehow, magically it seemed, everyone was clearly able to see the other's side. In the end, this group that had been close, and then seemingly divided, was now closer than ever. I couldn't quite believe what I had just witnessed.

We all went upstairs, and they invited me to sit quietly while everyone meditated for twenty minutes. A peace invaded the space that reminded me of childhood summers spent wandering through the old-growth forest behind my grandparents' weekend home, picking huckleberries. There was no place that I'd rather be.

When the meditation time ended, Nick asked me, "How was that?"

"Peaceful," I replied, with a smile I couldn't control.

Nick smiled back and asked if I still wanted to go to the meeting with them. Of course, I did! One of Nick's roommates, a guy named Kevin, also joined us, growing our group to about eight. We all drove down to the meeting hall. It was much more crowded than the meeting we had gone to that morning. There was a sign on the secretary's table that read "NO CLAPPING." No clapping? That seemed like a weird rule.

The meeting got underway and Kevin was asked to share. There was power in his words and in his voice. People couldn't contain themselves. Everyone was hooting and hollering, laughing and cheering. This very serious "no clapping" gathering had quickly gotten rowdy. One after the other, these people shared. There was humility, triumph, hope, and power in their words. I was so inspired. In the almost three years I had attended meetings, I had never experienced anything like this before. I knew there was something they were doing that I had never done. They said it was God, the twelve steps, and sponsorship. I had thought I knew what those things were, but it was pretty clear that whatever these people were doing was radically different than whatever I had ever done.

After the meeting, as we climbed the stairs to Nick's apartment, I asked him, "Will you show me what you do?"

"You mean the Steps? I'd love to."

He explained alcoholism in a way that was so simple and clear, then told me about his journey with God. He asked me if I believed I was an alcoholic and if I was willing to turn my life and will over to the care of God. He made it clear that if I said yes, he would only be my human sponsor, and that his job was to get me connected to God, the ultimate sponsor, as soon as possible so we could journey together side by side, not one above the other. He assured me that he was human and would probably let me down soon, if he hadn't already, and that he was not the one who was going to change my life.

I didn't really understand what "turning my life and will over to the care of God" looked like, but if it meant living with the freedom he had, I was willing to do anything.

We prayed together: "God, I offer myself to Thee, to build with me and to do with me as Thou will. Relieve me of the bondage of self that I may better do Thy will. Take away my difficulties, that victory over them would bear witness to Your power, Your love, and Your way of life."

After we prayed, Nick handed me a notebook and some pens. He outlined an inventory process and showed me how to take stock of my resentment, fear, and romantic relationships, instructing me to be thorough, fearless, and honest as I looked back over my life. He left me to write and went to bed, telling me to wake him up when I was done.

I never had been thorough, fearless, and honest in looking at my life. Even when trying to be honest, I had always left out details about my actions or feelings to me look a little less pathetic and a little more heroic than I had actually been. I was so terrified to look deep inside myself and confront all of that, and was even more terrified that someone else might find out how much self-doubt and self-loathing I actually had. But I knew that if I was ever going to be as free as Nick, I couldn't afford to hold anything back. I had decided that no matter what the personal cost might be, I was going to trust that God had me, because I had seen it work in Nick, and I had hope it would work for me too.

I wrote all night. Memories I had hidden away came to the surface. I wrote about shame I had carried around my father's alcoholism, my parents' divorce, and the sexual encounters I had as a child. All these things I hoped would never see the light of day now hung on me like anchors as I wrote them all down, yet I had a strong feeling that the pain they brought was going to be taken away.

As I looked at my unforgiveness and the fear behind it, I realized how much I had manufactured my own misery. I had placed my life in the hands of people, expecting them to be perfect and treat me perfectly. It was as though I had unconsciously written a script I expected everyone to follow, but had never given them a copy. Then, when they didn't follow the script, I resented them and blamed them for failing me while taking no responsibility for the confusion and hurt I was creating. As I wrote, I prayed for God to take all these things away, to mature me into a man who could serve instead of one who constantly demanded to be served.

When I had nothing more to write, I woke Nick up and shared it all with him. We talked for hours. I had never felt so free. When I was done, he told me to meditate for an hour on what I had done, and ask God to reveal to me anything I may have left out. He went down the street to get us bagels and coffee, and when he got back we prayed again, thanking God that with this new revelation, we knew Him and ourselves better. We asked Him to take all of it—the good and the bad—because what I thought had been good was not nearly as good as God intended, and what was bad was really so much worse than I thought. I asked God for a clean slate, and a power to be able to live it.

"My Creator, I'm now willing that You should have all of me, good and bad," I prayed, with Nick's guidance. "I pray that You now remove from me every single defect of character that stands in the way of my usefulness to You and my fellows. Grant me strength as I go out from here to do Your bidding. Amen."

As I shared my inventory, Nick had taken notes and compiled a list of relationships that needed amends. Many were people I had blamed when I was really the one at fault. Even in situations where I was only partly to blame, I needed to take responsibility for my part. He stressed the need to start on this right away, and to continue to use the inventory process we had just practiced to surrender fear and clean up any mistakes I'd make as I began to practice this examined way of life.

Nick also stressed the importance of meditation, which he called an internal house cleaning. He explained that, just like my actual house, my internal house would get messy if I didn't take an active role in keeping it clean. I might live in the most beautiful house in the world, but if I didn't hang up my clothes and towels, put away my shoes, make my bed, wash dishes, do laundry, dust, mop, sweep, and vacuum, in only a few days my beautiful house would become unlivable. I would avoid being there, eat out all the time, and only come home to sleep. When I woke up and saw the mess, I would want to leave again as quickly as possible. I wouldn't even think about inviting people over, limiting all my social interactions to activities outside the home.

But, if I took a Saturday and did a deep clean, scrubbed the dishes, did several loads of laundry, cleaned the counters, toilets, and floors, swept the decks, and put everything away in its proper place, I could then sit on the couch and relish my beautiful house. I would become grateful for what, just a few hours before, had been a great burden. My perspective would be reset, and I'd realize there's no place I'd rather be. Then, if I started cleaning messes as they come up, putting things away, and keeping the house clean, the gratitude that I had for it would deepen. I'd stay connected with others as well, having an open house as a hub for community. My time spent in gratitude on the couch would become more purposeful too, as I no longer simply enjoyed the relief of a clean house, but began dreaming of how this place could be even more wonderful as I invited more people to share the wonderful life God had given me. My gratitude for all that I had been given to share with others would grow.

Caring for my internal life was exactly the same, Nick urged. When I had disagreements that I didn't amend, conversations I didn't finish, issues I didn't address, and regrets I didn't share, things piled up internally, and the last thing I wanted to do was spend time with myself. I avoided myself, looking for distraction wherever I can find it. This opened all sorts of opportunity for behavior that brought regret and shame. It caused barriers in my relationships, and connections became shallow. But when I took the time to do a deep clean, like I did with the inventory I shared with Nick, my perspective was restored and I got to sit in gratitude for the life I've been given to steward. Immediately, my thoughts would turn to community and service to others.

This analogy made perfect sense to me. I had just done a major internal house cleaning. I had learned a process that unraveled the complicated mess of my life. It enabled me not only to clean up my unresolved emotional and relational issues, but to regain perspective. As a result, a fire had been lit inside me like the one I saw burning in Nick and his friends, a fire to share the thing I had just gotten. I trusted Nick when he said that continued inventory and meditation would broaden and deepen that ability. He offered to connect me with the woman who taught him to meditate, so I made an appointment the following month to meet her.

I decided to practice this new process of making amends with the friends who I had traveled with to San Francisco. I arranged to meet them for lunch, and guided the conversation so that I could individually and collectively make amends for my selfish and self-centered behavior—not just while I'd been actively drinking and using, but over the course of our friendships, some which I'd had since elementary school.

It turned out to be one of the most amazing afternoons. I had only known how to connect with friends through drinking. Now I was learning to connect though humility, vulnerability, and honesty, and it was so much more powerful than the connection I'd found through drinking, drugs, or sex. Best of all, it didn't end with regret—in fact, it didn't end at all. I knew it was the beginning of building more authentic friendships.

Instead of returning home to San Diego with those friends, I decided to stay in San Francisco for another few days to continue working with Nick and growing in community with the people I was meeting through him. At the first meeting I went to with Nick and my new friends, I was asked to share. I talked about my struggles, my time in recovery with no solution, and the incredible experience I had had over the past two days with God and this new group of friends. After the meeting, a young guy approached me asking for help. I invited him to dinner with us, and just like that our community grew.

After a week in the city, I headed back to San Diego. I went to a meeting my first day back, excited to bring light into the darkness. Thanks to my newfound experience, I imagined I'd be able to help others and the ones that I'd known in recovery would be overjoyed that I'd finally "got it." I was more excited than the older members of the group. Frustratingly, however, they didn't see my progress. It seemed like everyone already thought I was a little crazy, and now I was a little crazy about God and AA. I kept going, though, and soon, guys who were new, broken, and truly desperate for a solution began coming to me after meetings and asking for help. So, I worked with them, continuing to share with Nick the inventory of my resentment and fear and meditating twenty minutes in the morning and at night.

༶

I was now about three months sober. I headed up to Vancouver to visit my family, staying with my grandparents as usual. I hoped to see my father, Roland, who I hadn't talked to in two years, while I was there. He and I had reconnected when I got sober at sixteen and spent time together the following summer when I was seventeen, but I had gotten busy with school and work and stopped visiting. I was nervous to call him, but I had this tool of inventory and meditation, so I prayed, wrote, and then called. For privacy, I used the phone upstairs in my grandparents' room.

Soon after we began our conversation, I could tell by the tone of his voice that my dad had something on his mind. He has a thick French accent and gets very animated when he has something to say.

"Morganu, listen," he said. "You are nineteen. You are a man. You have your whole life ahead of you. You are smart, you are good looking, you can do anything you want to. Why do you think you need a 'dad'? 'Dad' is who raised you. I am your father, but I am not your 'dad.' Your mom, she goofed us. I never got to be your 'dad' and now I'm old and have nothing for you. I have nothing to give you and you have everything ahead of you. You are a man. Stand on your feet. You need nobody. So, Morganu, I think it's better you don't call me again, okay? Never call me again. You remind me of the failure of my life, okay? So don't call. Okay? I love you, Morganu. Goodbye."

I was heartbroken. I wanted to say, "I don't need you to parent me. I just want to know you and know where I'm from."

As I sat in shock and in grief, the phone rang. I answered, hoping he'd reconsidered. Instead, I heard, "Morganu, listen. I'm serious. I don't want you to think I'm not serious. I want you to know, don't ever call again. Am I clear? Don't ever call me. Okay, Morganu. I love you. Don't call, okay? Bye."

I wanted to scream "F**k you!" as loud as I could. Instead, I picked up the phone and called Nick. I'd gotten in the habit of calling him every day, not always for advice, but to share my fears and my resentments to be accountable. And Nick held me accountable. He wouldn't take my call just to chat. If I didn't have an inventory to share, he'd tell me to call him back when I did.

By the time Nick answered the phone, I was sobbing. "Nick, it's Morgan. I called my dad. He told me, he told me to never call him again, and he hung up on me."

"Hey, hey," Nick interrupted. "Listen—did you take inventory?"

"Yes, right before I called him."

"Did you take inventory after you called him?"

"No, I just called you."

"Listen," Nick said, "I don't have any experience with this, but I have a ton of experience with inventory. So why don't you take inventory and call me back." With a click, he hung up.

I couldn't believe it. I stared at the phone. Are you kidding me? What an insensitive a**hole. I went from being incredibly sad to incredibly angry. I started stomping around the room, trying to thing of some clever way I could call him back and tell him off. How dare he! I was pissed. Suddenly, excruciating pain erupted in one of my feet. I collapsed and grabbed my foot, trying to see what had happened. I discovered that I had stomped right on top of a sewing needle that had been dropped on the carpet. It was buried about an inch and a half into my foot, and I knew I needed pliers to get it out. I crawled over to a dresser and found tools. Finally, with some work, I managed to get the needle out.

The dresser where I found the pliers also had a pad of paper and a pen. My foot was throbbing and I didn't have it in me to keep pouting, so I decided I'd take inventory. I didn't know what I was going to write, but as I put pen to paper, all the resentment, fear, and shame around my relationship with my father started to bubble up. I wrote and wrote and wrote. Almost ten pages later, the pen slowed down and I couldn't think of another thing. Then I called Nick. I shared it all with him, and he shared with me. We talked, cried, and laughed. In fact, about fifteen minutes into our call, I laughed so hard I fell off the bed.

When we were done talking, I went to sit in meditation. Somehow, peace and joy came over me. When I got up, I couldn't wait to get to a meeting to try and find someone I could encourage. (If that's not a miracle of God, I don't know what is. I know people who have spent years in therapy to achieve less—and don't get me wrong, I'm not knocking therapy.) I couldn't believe how free I felt. I wasn't angry at my father. I pitied him. I also trusted that God had a plan.

It was a beautiful, late-summer evening and I walked to the meeting. I was asked to share, and after the meeting, I served some guys who were newly sober. I took one of those guys, Dave, out to coffee with the rest of the group. We laughed and joked into the night. Sitting in the restaurant laughing and talking just a few hours after that painful phone call gave me a glimpse of how it could be possible to navigate life sober, even on a day where I felt my heart would break. It gave me hope. It was the first of many experiences that would teach me that finding fellowship with God and others in the midst of the worst situations was the key to success in sobriety, and really in life. Not one of us are given a "get out of all of life's problems free" card. But if I let Him, God was more than able to take the worst and most impossible situation and use it for good.

Nick remained my sponsor for two and a half years. I called him nearly every day and visited him and the rest of the fellowship in San Francisco as often as I could. Then Nick got married and started a family. One day I called to share inventory, and he told me he couldn't listen to my inventory because he hadn't taken his own that morning. Nick was always conscientious about not relying on yesterday's revelation. If he hadn't taken and shared inventory himself that day, he wouldn't just wing it with me. First, he'd get right with God and man, and then pour out into me. I told him I'd call him back and asked how much time he needed. Then he said he didn't need time. He and his wife had decided to leave AA and focus more on their relationship with God in a church setting. He said he'd be happy to recommend me to someone else in the fellowship, and hoped we'd remain friends, but he could no longer be my AA sponsor.

I was crushed. I took inventory about Nick, called another member of the fellowship, and shared it, but it wasn't the same. I didn't know what to do. I wasn't interested in joining Nick in his church escapades, and I didn't want another sponsor. Nick had always been clear that I was not supposed to rely on him, that he would only let me down, and that my reliance had to be on God. Now I was being put to the test, and it became pretty clear that I had relied on Nick and his relationship with God rather than solidifying my own. My taking inventory and meditation had been more about building my relationship with Nick than building a relationship with God. The practice was effective, but my motivation was flawed, and at the time I just couldn't see it. I didn't want to be judged for not having a sponsor, so I asked someone in the fellowship in San Diego. But it wasn't the same. Before long, I started cutting corners in every area of my life

CHAPTER 4:
The Bondage of Freedom

During the time that Nick was my sponsor, I joined a young people's home group. It was a great place to be of service, because it attracted people who were just getting sober and in a similar season of life. I got involved with running the group, found community with other members, and became a respected member.

When I was a year-and-a-half sober, I started dating a girl named Michele I met at the group, who had just passed the one-year mark of sobriety. We started sleeping together on our first date. We dated for six months, but it was a tumultuous relationship—we broke up and got back together more times than I could count. She was my first real relationship, and I opened my heart up to her. Several times she said to me, "I don't believe I have the capacity to love another human being." I would always assure her that she did. But fractures in the relationship surfaced when she began to cheat. The pattern was always the same. She would cheat, blame me for her cheating, we would reconcile, and she would cheat again. It went on like this for months, and in the process my heart was systematically shredded and eventually started to harden—not just against her, but against women.

On multiple occasions after Michele and I broke up, I went out and had a string of one-night stands, trying to find relief from my pain in the arms of another woman. I thought retaliation would bring me peace, but it just brought more pain. The women I slept with didn't look at me as a fun, one-night encounter, but as Mr. Happily-Ever-After. I hated seeing the pain, shame, and disappointment in their eyes when they realized there was no future with me, and that they had only been used for sex. I never went out with the intention of hurting anyone. I was longing for real connection, but I had no idea how to create it. When I went out dancing, met a girl, and ended up back at her place or mine, the furthest thing from my mind was hurting her or myself. I genuinely was open to having a relationship, but as soon as we slept together I was filled with such a deep sense of shame that I wanted to get as far away as possible. I hated the way it made me feel.

During one of the especially bad breakups with Michele, I let myself be seduced by a man. I was feeling completely weak and worthless and wanted someone to want me. I let him give me oral sex and he told me I didn't need to reciprocate. I left my self-esteem on the floor and threw up on the way back to my car.

It's a strange thing when pleasure and shame mix together. The physical act felt good, and there was emotional satisfaction in being desired, even worshiped. It gave me a feeling of power over someone when I was feeling most powerless. But there was also a profound feeling of shame in what I had allowed someone to do to me. Even though I hated it, and hated myself for doing it, there was something that pulled me back to it a few more times over the course of several months.

I was a fan of electronic music and went out to clubs regularly, which is where I'd meet girls. A couple of them turned into more than a one-night stand. There was a girl I'd call on a Saturday night if I was back from the club, lonely and unable to sleep. I let her see me at my most vulnerable and confided in her. I liked having her around when I needed her, but I was ashamed of the nature of our relationship, so I never invited her to join me and my friends the next morning for our weekly Sunday brunch.

One Saturday night, I called her at 2:30 in the morning to see if she wanted to come over. She asked why I never asked her to brunch with my friends and if I was ashamed of her. I told her I wasn't, and that if she wanted to go to brunch with us in the morning, I'd love to have her come. In the moment, I truly meant it. But after she came over and we had sex, I was suddenly filled with dread at the idea of having her meet my friends. I wanted her to leave, but I knew that would devastate her. I tried to hide how I was feeling, but I was so awkward that she realized the truth and confronted me.

"I know you don't want me here," she said. "I don't know what the f**k is wrong with you. I don't think you have a f**king clue who you are or what you want. I hope you figure yourself out—not for yourself, but so you don't hurt anyone else like this. Don't ever call me again." Then she stormed out.

I was relieved she had left, but her words haunted me as I lay awake that night. What the f**k was wrong with me? Was she right? Did I not know myself? I really didn't want to hurt anyone, and it killed me to see the pain in the eyes of these girls. I felt like such a hypocrite. I knew how it felt to be so betrayed and hurt, and now I was the one hurting others.

Maybe Michele was right—maybe it was all my fault. Maybe I'd never figure women out. All I seemed to do was cause pain. The more I thought about it, the more I concluded that I was a failure at relationships with women. Then I thought, Maybe it would be easier to be gay. It wasn't really what I wanted, but maybe I just didn't know myself. I never felt like any of the men I had been with regretted the experience like the women did. I decided to give it a try.

I had some gay friends and arranged to meet them at a gay club the next Saturday night. Being there quickly felt like freedom. Everyone was incredibly accepting and encouraging, and I felt like I didn't need to hide anything from anyone. My friends introduced me to their friends, and almost overnight, it seemed, I knew everyone in the gay community in San Diego. Soon, I was getting invited to lots of parties, brunches, dinners, clubs, and trips, and quickly making new friends.

One friend, Travis, became my workout partner and confidante. I told him all about Michele and how after all we'd been through, I still loved her. Travis said that love shouldn't have a gender—it should just be two people who love each other. I liked that idea.

However, I soon encountered realities in the gay community that were strange, uncomfortable, or didn't seem quite so safe, free, or accepting. While some of the events to which people invited me were fairly innocuous, many involved sex and drugs. I attended many seemingly normal parties that quickly devolved into sex parties. Drugs, especially meth, were plentiful in the club scene and at after-parties, and I made several awkward getaways from partiers trying to offer them to me.

At one point, a man I had seen out at the clubs began sending me sexually explicit instant messages. He was half of a gay married couple who were very politically active and prominent in the community. The couple had an adopted son, and were actively fighting for marriage rights. When I tried to dodge his advances by asking him about his husband or their child, he explained that they had an open marriage. I didn't understand why anyone fighting for equality in marriage would want a marriage to be open. However, over time I discovered that almost all the couples I met in the gay community had open relationships.

One new friend sent me a discouraging email after attempting suicide. He was twenty-seven and felt like he was too old and not rich enough to get a boyfriend. "Everyone wants you when you're fresh meat," he wrote "You come into the scene at nineteen or twenty and feel like the world just opened up to you. You're young and pretty and everyone wants you around. You get invited to all the parties and the older rich guys buy you gifts and invite you on lavish trips. Everything has strings, but you don't care much because you're having the time of your life. But then twenty-five comes, and you're not as young and pretty as you were and you're not fresh meat anymore. There are two types of people in the gay community in San Diego—young and pretty, or old and rich. If you're young and pretty, you better hope you can make some money so that when you're old you can buy someone young and pretty. Because no one wants you when you're old and poor."

That letter hit me hard. I knew that he was cynical and had just lost a relationship, but I had seen firsthand the truth in what he said. I had even read a front-page article in the Gay and Lesbian Times addressing ageism in the gay community, accusing the community of essentially the same thing my friend had written about in his email.

I also had a hairdresser who lived a double life. Monday through Thursday, he was a family man who lived in a beautiful home with his beautiful wife and two daughters, and was seen as a pillar of his community. But Friday through Sunday, he took guys home to a separate apartment after nights out at the gay clubs. I always wondered if his wife knew, or if she believed he was out of town on business. The whole situation seemed so strange and sad to me.

One day, I was sitting in his chair getting my hair cut when he paused, looked me square in the eye, and said, "I've seen you."

"I know . . . I see you all the time," I said.

"No. I've seen you, and I know what you're doing. If you keep it up, one day you won't be able to do anything else."

I looked back at him and saw sadness and desperation in his eyes. It terrified me. I knew he had seen me out at the clubs just as I had seen him. Maybe he saw something in me that he saw in himself. Maybe he hated what he'd become. Maybe, like my friend Sam, who had been a catalyst to save me from suicide many years before, God was using a very broken vessel to save me from going down a dark path. All I know is that he put the fear of God in me.

That same week, I got a call from Michele. She had gotten a job at a graphic design firm and said she wanted to talk shop with me over lunch. I hadn't seen her in the six months that I had been in the gay scene. I picked her up from her office and we drove to a nice restaurant with a private table on their garden patio. Before I could even sit down, she said, "I've got to ask you a question, and you've got to be honest with me."

"Okay," I said as I took my chair. "What?"

"Well, a bunch of our friends from the young people's meeting have told me that they've see you out in Hillcrest around the gay clubs. Are you bisexual?"

"I guess you could say that," I admitted. "Sure."

"Great. I am too. I took a girl home last night."

"Wait . . . what?" I was dumbfounded, but also excited. There was a side to each of us that we had never shared with one another.

We had the best conversation we'd ever had, I thought. As I sat at that table talking, I felt closer to her than ever. Afterwards, we got in the car to drive back to her office. About two blocks from the office we stopped and had sex in the car. She told me she wanted to get back together, and I agreed. I didn't know what to think about what was happening, but I felt like I'd been in a fog, and suddenly sunlight had broken through.

I couldn't wait to introduce Michele to my new friends. I told her she had to come out the next night to the club, promising her that the gay clubs were so much more fun than the clubs we went to downtown and at the beach. There were no egos, and everyone was just there to dance and have a good time.

The next night, we got to the club early. I had told Travis, who had become my best friend, that there was someone that I wanted him to meet. When he showed up, Michele and I were dancing in a way that made it clear that she and I were together. Travis walked up to us, looked at me, and asked coldly, "Who the f**k is this?"

"This is Michele—the girl I told you about," I grinned. "We had the most amazing honest conversation we'd ever had at lunch yesterday, and we got back together."

"Did you tell her you were gay?"

"Travis, you know I've never said I was gay. I've thought I was bisexual, but you know I never stopped loving her. I thought you'd be happy for me. Haven't you always said that love shouldn't have a gender?"

Travis threw his drink on me and snapped, "Go back in the closet, Mary." Then he turned and walked away.

I didn't understand. Wasn't this community based on honesty, being true to oneself, and diversity? However, I soon discovered that many of the great new "friends" I had made shared Travis's attitude about me being back with Michele. I stayed with her, though, caring more about her than them not wanting anything to do with me.

But Michele and I didn't last. One day she told me that we either needed to get married or break up, and that she wasn't ready for marriage, so she thought we should take a break. She said she just needed to figure herself out outside of a relationship. I told her I'd give her whatever space and time she needed. Within a week, she was in another relationship.

Whenever Michele had told me, "I don't know if I'm actually capable of loving another human being," I had always encouraged her that she was, listing ways that I'd seen her show care and compassion. But seeing how quickly she went from saying we should get married to being in the arms of another man, I wondered, Who was this woman I had loved? Who was I? Have I been dating a sociopath?

I was the one who needed to figure themselves out outside of a relationship. In fact, there was a lot of work I needed to do. First, I needed to find an AA sponsor and mentor who I trusted as much as I had trusted Nick.

My friend Steve suggested I talk to a man named Will, whom I had known since I got sober. I went to hear Will speak at a large meeting, and as I listened to him, I felt like he was telling my story. After the meeting, I went up to thank him for sharing and he invited me out to dinner with a group of his friends.

At the restaurant, as we were waiting to order, someone asked me what had been going on in my life. I didn't really want to get into the whole sordid mess, but I talked a little about Michele. When I was finished, Will, who was sitting across from me, asked, "Can I take your inventory? I'll sign my own name to it." This meant that he would call me out, but not on anything that he also wasn't guilty of at some point in his life. Then he added, "I wouldn't bet on your continued sobriety." He went on to describe my life completely in a way that he couldn't possibly have known unless he had been through the exact same things. I was dumbfounded.

Will and I talked for hours in the parking lot after dinner. It had been a long time since I related to anyone as much as I did to him. I asked him to sponsor me, told him it had been quite a while since I'd taken inventory, and admitted I had a whole lot I needed to look at. He gave me a week to write the inventory. We met the following Saturday evening at his house and ended up talking all night. I shared inventory, and he shared stories from his past that mirrored mine.

Will was wonderful. He had a wife and two young sons, and I immediately felt adopted into their family. He was also incredibly encouraging. After I shared my inventory, which included the worst things I had ever done, he told me, "If you could have done any better, you would have, and when you can, you will."

I believed him. If he was like me—and I believed he was—and could get to where he was from where I'd been, there was hope for me.

I had a lot of hope after sharing that inventory. There's a ton of freedom that comes with sharing burdens you've been carrying for years with someone who understands from experience. At that point, I became much more comfortable with sharing the worst of my past, and I started mentoring several young men in AA who had similar pasts, becoming pretty close with two of them, Thomas and Forrest. I had known Thomas since I was sixteen, and Forrest I had known for just a few years. They were good friends.

Then, one night, Forrest jokingly pointed a gun he didn't know was loaded at Thomas and fired. Thomas was killed, and Forrest was arrested. Forrest used his one call to phone me from the holding cell at the police station. He told me he'd killed Thomas, and asked me to call his mother to tell her what he had done and that he was sorry. I was in shock. I had never been asked to do something like that, but I numbly made the call. I made a lot of calls—calling in favors to get Forrest a lawyer and money to post bail, and trying my best to show up and be strong for our group of friends.

Forrest and Thomas were central figures in our young people's recovery fellowship. As details about Thomas' death were revealed during the course of Forrest's preliminary hearings, that tight group of young people in recovery became completely divided. The District Attorney charged Forrest with first-degree murder and the case went to trial. Forrest was acquitted on all counts, but went into hiding after people from our formerly close group threatened his life.

I felt like I needed to keep the group from falling apart, and pushed down my feelings of sadness, disappointment, and loss. My sponsor Will was a constant source of encouragement, but both of us were indulging in unhealthy behavior in our lives to cope with realities over which we felt we had no control—relationship problems, spending problems, and situations in our lives that left us emotionally wrecked. I was comfortable sharing everything with him, and he shared his worst with me, but though sharing left us feeling a little lighter, our behavior didn't change much. We were like the blind leading the blind.

With so much feeling out-of-control around me I started looking for areas where I could regain some control in my personal life. I wanted to get back in shape physically, and I thought when I did that mental and spiritual health would follow. I started going to Bikram Yoga. The classes were 90 minutes long in a crowded, humid room heated to 120°. The practice was hard too, it wasn't peaceful stretching, it was more like bootcamp with drill-sergeants in spandex screaming directions at the class—it took everything in me just to make it through. The feeling after class though was endorphin fueled euphoria. Even though the class was tough, the feeling after was incredible. I became obsessed and started going to two classes a day. As my body started to transform through rigorous exercise, I decided to adopt a healthier diet too. I was introduced to organic raw-food veganism by a friend, and decided to go all in.

Raw-food vegans believe that heat kills the natural enzymes in plants that aid with their digestion. By not heating food above 115 degrees, the enzymes stay intact. I loved to cook, and took on gourmet raw-foodism as a new obsession, preparing delicious healthy meals for all my friends. I thought for sure this new path was going to be the answer, but even as my body got healthier on the outside, there were still things inside me that were unsettled. My sponsor Will and I would talk about art, philosophy, and balance, but the people around us could see what we were blind to—that in reality both of our lives were still pretty unbalanced.

Eventually, Will's marriage ended, and soon after, Will relapsed, abusing a prescription medication his doctor had given him for depression. Even though Will had relapsed, he never left the fellowship. He just changed his sobriety date and started over. I insisted on keeping him as my sponsor. I gave him a 90-day token the same night he gave me a 9-year cake.

CHAPTER 5:
No Matter Where You Go, There You Are

I met Bre at a young people's recovery convention in Denver. She was from Aspen. After the convention, we started talking on the phone almost every night. She was so easy to talk to, and within a few weeks it seemed like we knew everything about each other's lives. I thought if our relationship was even going to have a chance to get off the ground, I'd have to tell her everything about my past. I did, and to my surprise, she didn't run away screaming. Instead, my transparency and her acceptance made us feel even closer.

Before long, Bre came to visit me in San Diego. I wanted to introduce her to my parents. My mom, who was an excellent chef, invited us over for dinner. As Mom was preparing dinner, Bre and I looked through albums of me as a baby. She saw a picture of me with my French father, Roland, who is 5'6", black-haired, and olive-skinned. I am 6'3" with blonde hair and blue eyes. As a baby, my hair was almost white, and I had pink skin.

"Who's that?" she asked.

"That's my dad," I answered.

"Are you sure?" she laughed, incredulous. "He doesn't look anything like you. You sure your mom wasn't getting a little 'something something' on the side?"

I was shocked. "Of course, I'm sure. This is the first time you're meeting my parents and you're asking me if I know who my father is?"

I stuck my head into the kitchen where my mom was putting the final touches on dinner. Jokingly, I asked, "Hey Mom, are you sure Roland's my dad? I don't look anything like him. You sure it wasn't the mailman or the milkman?"

My mom looked at me like she'd seen a ghost.

Geez, I thought, can't she take a joke? "Hey, I'm kidding," I assured her. "I know I take after your side."

The experience made me think about Roland, though. There was so much I didn't know about him. I was past the point of wanting him to be my dad, but I felt in some ways that because I didn't know him, I didn't really know myself.

About a year later, I decided to write Roland a letter telling him the story of my life from the age of four to the present. I thought if I was really honest with him about my struggles with alcoholism and addiction, maybe, hopefully, it would help him finally look at himself and his demons. The letter was twenty-seven typed pages. I tried my hardest to make it an open-hearted invitation into a relationship—not as a son who needed a daddy, but as a man who wanted to know his father as a friend. As I sent it off, I prayed that it would be received well.

About two weeks later, I got a call from him. "Morgan! I cannot believe your mother. I knew she was bad, but I had no idea. I knew she goofed me, but she goofed you too. She should be arrested." He went on and on about how terrible my mother was and how she had destroyed everyone's life. He took no responsibility for himself, couldn't see any of the good in my life, and completely missed my heart in writing the letter.

I was dumbfounded. I prayed, "God, if you want him to be in my life, You're going to have to work it out, because I'm done."

Around the same time, my mom went to a week-long personal development course in the Bay Area. I called her the night she got back to ask her how it was. She said, "It was great. But listen . . . I have something I need to tell you, and I'd like to do it in person. It's a family secret."

"Sure, why don't you come over tomorrow for dinner," I suggested. "I'll make food and we can go for a walk on the beach and talk."

The next evening I prepared a raw food, vegan feast—two kinds of raw ravioli, an heirloom tomato salad, and a raw blueberry torte for dessert. I had just put out dinner when I heard the doorbell ring. I opened the door and found my mom standing there, her face full of fear and turmoil, like a little girl who had just crashed her father's car. I'd never seen her look the way she did that night.

"Come in!" I urged her. "Dinner's ready."

She shook her head. "I think I'd better stay outside. You might not want to eat with me after I tell you what I need to tell you."

"Mom, you could tell me you got into a fight with the neighbors, killed them, stashed their bodies in your trunk, and you need to ditch the car and the bodies and get out of the country, and I would still want to eat with you before I helped you escape."

"It's worse than that."

I thought, Holy s**t! I literally just thought of the worst possible scenario I could think of. What could possibly be worse than that?

"Kent Warmington is your father," she said, wincing as though expecting me to slam the door in her face.

"That's great!" I replied, pulling her into a huge hug.

Kent was a friend of my mom's from college. I had known him as a young boy when we lived in Vancouver. I remembered that he was always nice to me and that I'd liked him, though I hadn't seen him since we had moved.

"You're not mad?" she asked.

"No," I replied. "I'm relieved. Roland has always been such an a**hole. I'm so glad I'm not his son."

My mom went on to explain that about a year before I was born, Roland's alcoholism had gotten out of control. She had left France and returned to Vancouver for the winter to get her head straight and figure out whether she could muster the will to stay in her marriage. While she was in Vancouver, she met up with her friend Kent, whose marriage had also fallen apart. One thing led to another and they slept together.

Disgusted with herself, she had returned to France to reconcile with her husband. During the time she should have had her period, she experienced some light bleeding and thought there was no way she could have been pregnant by Kent. She didn't know that when an embryo attaches itself to the wall of the uterus, sometimes there is what's called implantation bleeding because the embryo breaks a blood vessel. When she missed her next period after reconciling with Roland, she figured that the baby must be his. In fact, she had believed that until the night Bre came over and I popped my head into the kitchen and asked with a smirk, "Hey Mom, are you sure Roland's my dad?" She said my smirk was exactly Kent's smirk. She hadn't believed it possible, but she researched implantation bleeding, and she realized the truth. All these years, all that pain—how could she have missed something so obvious? She worried I would disown her and that her husband and my brother would reject her as a whore. So she carried that secret for two years, until she couldn't anymore

I vaguely knew something had been going on with her during those two years. She had become almost religiously judgmental, making comments whenever she heard people swear or witnessed other offensive behavior. I had wondered what had gotten into her, and now I knew—it had been shame. I knew what it was like to carry shame, and I just hugged her. My love for my mom actually grew.

That night, after a long, deep, incredible talk with my mom over dinner, I looked up Kent on the internet. His number was unlisted, but I found his brother and sister-in-law. I called them the next morning.

A woman answered, "Hello?"

"Uh, hi, is this Margaret Warmington?"

"Yes. Who's this?"

"My name is Morgan. I think you might know my mother, Kathy. You would have known her as Kathy Stéphan. She was a friend of Kent Warmington's."

"Yes, I remember her. How can I help you?"

"Well, it's a bit of a long, weird story . . ."

I went on to tell her what had happened. When I finished, she said, "Well, that sounds like Kent. You know, he's coming over for dinner tonight. Would you like me to give him a message?"

I gave her my number and my mom's number, as I thought Kent might like to talk to her first. He called her that night. Three days later, he flew from Vancouver to San Diego to meet me.

I went to meet him at the airport. At the rental car counter, the agent asked him, "Would you like to put your son here as a second driver?"

"My son?" Kent asked. "What makes you think he's my son?"

The agent looked at me, looked at him, rolled her eyes and laughed as if to say, "You'd be a fool not to notice how much you look like each other." We did.

Getting to know Kent was the craziest thing. We shared interests and mannerisms that I didn't share with anyone else in my family. As I discovered more about him and his history, so much about my life began to make sense. Kent was wonderful and engaging, and the part of my life that was missing with Roland finally felt like it had been found.

※

On the outside, my life looked great. I was making lots of money, driving a fancy new car, in a relationship with a great girl, and living in an awesome house I had just been approved for a loan to buy. I also did yoga every day and was a vegan raw-foodist eating, what was in my mind, the healthiest diet on the planet. But something was off. I started to experience low-level anxiety frequently and had a hard time sleeping. I'd find myself up at two or three in the morning, watching this woman who loved me sleep and feeling a million miles away from her and from my life. The idea of buying this house seemed so overwhelming. Marriage seemed overwhelming. Everything seemed overwhelming.

My company sent me to New York on a two-month assignment to work with a licensing group, grow our brand, and bring it into some of the largest retail chains in the country. I worked intensely for the first six weeks, designing products to grow our line. The whole time, my anxiety got worse, until one morning on the way to work, I had a full-blown panic attack in the middle of Times Square. I got in a cab and asked the driver to take me to my hotel near Columbus Circle. He must have misheard me, however, because he took me to Chinatown. Times Square has to be one of the worst places in the world to have a panic attack, but a close second has got to be Canal Street with all its fake purses, smells, and street vendors. I couldn't be in a car anymore, however, so I walked seventy-two blocks back to my hotel. By the time I got there, the panic attack was over.

I called in sick to work so I could take the day to figure myself out. I decided that I could finish my assignment remotely, and that I needed to go back home and do a juice cleanse. It was the city's fault. Manhattan wasn't a healthy place. I'd get back on track with my diet and exercise. That would fix it.

I went home and went on the Master cleanse—that's the lemon juice, cayenne pepper, maple syrup, and water cleanse—for a month. I was already skinny, but a month of that left me at 6'3" and 148 lbs. In my mind, I was ripped. It was true that I had no body fat, but I was ripped in a prisoner-of-war kind of way. It wasn't a good look.

During that cleanse, I made some decisions about my life. I decided not to accept the loan to buy the house I was living in, which was way out of my price range. I broke up with my girlfriend. That could have gone really badly, but she knew it was coming and had been preparing herself for it while I was in New York. I also quit my job and returned the car they had given me. Lastly, I decided to leave San Diego and live in an Essene Jewish raw-food, vegan spiritual community called Tree of Life in the high desert of Arizona. This was the ace up my sleeve. I had long thought that if my material existence didn't work out, I'd go be a monk—just not a Christian monk, because in my mind, Christians were small-minded, hypocritical, and believed in fairy tales.

I had become really interested in the life of Jesus, but I thought of him as a prophet, not God in the flesh. I hadn't read the Bible, but I had read countless books about Him, including The Gospel According to Jesus by Stephen Mitchell and The Life and Times of Jesus of Nazareth by Thomas Jefferson, and considered myself an expert on the subject. I even bought the Jefferson-Adams letters because I wanted to see what Thomas Jefferson and John Adams thought of Jesus. I also had several different translations of the Dead Sea scrolls. I was also interested in the life of John the Baptist, who was my inspiration for going to live in an Essene Jewish community.

The Tree of Life community was started by Gabriel Cousens, a Jewish rabbi, Essene priest, and the most credentialed expert on vegetarian nutrition on the planet. He started his medical practice believing that his God-given purpose on earth was to help people clear out and heal their bodies so that they could better commune with God. The practice attracts mostly people healing from diseases, celebrities wanting a detox retreat, and wealthy people who want to live forever.

I sold off or stored all my worldly possessions and moved to Tree of Life, hoping it would bring the change I was seeking. I was obsessed with healthy eating and dreamed of opening a raw food restaurant. I thought I could go there, get my master's degree in vegan, live-food nutrition, make myself perfect through yoga, spirituality, and healthy eating, and iron out the other details later.

Hope is a funny thing. When you have no experience with something, it's easy to believe theoretically that a thing is possible. I'd never lived the life of a monk. I had never been 100% strictly organic, vegan, and raw. I'd been close, but I hadn't been balanced. I hadn't had a daily practice with yoga while 100% devoted to this balanced "healthy" diet, and I hadn't lived in a community where everyone had a strict spiritual practice. I hoped that if I could engage myself completely in these three areas, I would be able to "overcome the world," just like Jesus did. I saw Christ as a man who had lived really well, someone who had "figured it out." I thought He had overcome the world in His own human power, and that I could do the same.

I moved to Arizona dreaming that it would be the total and complete answer to all my problems. And it started off amazingly. It was beautiful. The community was filled with fascinating people, and I seemed to fit right in. I met many people in transition, many of whom had accomplished a lot in their lives—a former supermodel, the former head designer for Barbie from Mattel, a celebrity nutritionist. I quickly made friends and stayed up late into the night talking with them, dreaming about a utopian existence free from problems and worldly concerns.

I apprenticed in the kitchen, learning from great minds how to prepare amazing food. Morning and evening, we participated in fire ceremonies and meditation. Wednesday evenings, we performed a Hindu call-and-response chanting called Kirtan. We spent all Friday preparing for Shabbat, the Jewish Sabbath day, which we observed from sundown Friday to sundown Saturday, fasting and enjoying community. It was a wonderful time and the highlight of the week. The Sabbath closed with the Havdalah ceremony, which involved teaching, singing, and dancing. It was wonderful. I was "all in." Well . . . I was mostly in. It was wonderful and new, and I was fully distracted with the wonder and newness of it all. Little by little, I started to be able to imagine life there, and I thought it would be happy. It was beautiful, the food was amazing, and there was no shortage of interesting people—that's all you need, right?

One day, Gabriel and his wife Shanti invited me over for dinner. I was excited because that was a rare honor to be invited to dine with them. They told me they believed that God had brought me to the community to be their head of marketing and branding, and offered to ship my belongings to Arizona, give me a rent-free house, and pay me a small salary while I continued through their master's program. I think they had Googled me and found out that I had been an accomplished advertising creative director with a background in branding. The community was funded primarily from the proceeds of Gabriel's medical practice and the sales of his books, retreats, and speaking gigs. Their branding was terrible, and I did have an opinion about how they could improve it. On one level, their offer seemed like a dream come true, but on another, it didn't sit right with me. I had run away from doing that kind of work and wasn't interested in going back to my career, which I blamed for my misery. Nevertheless, I accepted their offer.

I went back to San Diego, where everything I owned was sitting in a one-year, prepaid storage unit, loaded up the truck with my art, electronics, designer wardrobe, massive record collection, and modern furniture, and moved it all out to a tiny house two miles outside Patagonia, Arizona (population 400). But almost as soon as I got everything moved in, I realized I had made a huge mistake.

When I first moved to Arizona, I had brought only a single, large suitcase that represented my mood at the time—vegan, spiritual, minimalist. This was one facet of who I was—the one I thought was right, and the one I wanted to preserve. Now that all my stuff was there—beautiful, curated, and perfectly arranged—the other facets of my life were staring me in the face. Someone once said, "No matter where you go, there you are." Walking away from most of my life and putting the rest in a storage unit couldn't change who I truly was. I realized I couldn't escape myself, not in that way. I also realized I didn't want to.

As this truth hit home, the ramifications of what I had done started to become real to me. I had walked away from a huge salary and made a ton of sacrifices to go "be spiritual," and now I was making one-sixth of my former salary living in the middle of nowhere. I had also left my job with no severance and burnt through savings paying off the last six months of the lease on my house and depreciation on my car, as well as buying all the books for the master's program and six-month apprenticeship. I was broke. Even if I wanted to leave, now I couldn't afford to. Clearly, I had not planned this out very well. What was I thinking?

As I was struggling with this revelation, my great-aunt invited my family to spend Christmas with her in Colonial Williamsburg. I flew home to San Diego for a day so we could fly as a family out to the East Coast. The night I flew home, I ran into a sober friend of mine named Christine, who seemed thrilled to see me.

"Where have you been, Morgan?" she asked. "We've been trying to get a hold of you for months, but no one knew where you were. We started a clothing line and need branding. You need to quit what you're doing and come work with us!"

Christine told me all about the project that she and her husband had started with an artist named Pete—streetwear meets art, but with soul. It sounded incredible. They offered to move me back to San Diego, let me live in the guest house on their estate, and give me free use of a car.

It seemed too good to be true. Could I just leave? What would Gabriel and Shanti do? I told Christine that I'd think about it, and did just that the entire time I was in Virginia. At the end of the trip, I flew back to Arizona. I knew I needed to leave the community, but I was scared. What if this was just another way for me to try to escape? I wanted to be sure I wasn't running from a bad situation, but going to a good one.

There was a woman at Tree of Life who was Christian and worked as a housekeeper. People said she was psychic, but you couldn't just go up to her and ask her to tell you your fortune. From time to time, though, she got a "word" for people.

One day, she came up to me as I was washing up at the end of a long dinner shift in the kitchen. "Hey, I think I have something for you," she said. "Can you meet me tomorrow at noon?"

"Sure," I said.

"Good," she said. "Come with three questions that you wanted to have answered."

I had heard from everyone in the community that this woman's gift was really special, and something that she didn't share with many people. I was honored. I took her invitation seriously and spent time that night pondering which questions I wanted to ask her. But every question I thought of led me back to one: "What am I supposed to do with my life?" There's got to be another one, at least, I thought. But I literally couldn't bring another question to mind.

At noon the next day, we met me and went outside to a secluded space away from everyone eating lunch.

"Did you think of your three questions?" she asked.

"Well . . ."

She cut me off. "You could only think of one, huh?"

"Yeah, how did you know?"

"I see in pictures and scenes, but sometimes I doubt myself. I asked a question I already knew the answer to, just to make sure. You want to know what you're supposed to do with the rest of your life."

"How did you know?"

"I just do. I saw it. You ever consider being a pastor?"

I'd always had a love for people, and no matter how hard I tried to not lead, people had always followed me. For years in recovery, I had mentored and taught. But pastors were Christians, and to me Christians believed in fairy tales. With so many faiths in the world, all of them with faults, how could I pick just one?

"Yes. I've thought about that a ton, but I hate the idea of putting God in a box."

She looked at me and smiled. "Oh, honey, you need to reconsider what you think a pastor does."

That reply hit me. I suddenly wondered if my perspective was completely backwards. What if a pastor's job was actually to take God out of the box, to show Him real and alive to their congregation? What if I'd been wrong?

I started to get choked up and walked away from her to the labyrinth. Tree of Life had the largest Chartres labyrinth in the world. If you walked mindfully, it could take three hours to reach the center and walk back out. It did for me that day, and I wept the entire time. I hadn't had an emotional release like that in years. I was more unsure about what the future looked like than ever, but strangely I also had a peace about it.

When I got back to the house, I had a message from a friend from Vancouver: "There's a young people's recovery conference happening this weekend in Mexico, a few hours south of where you are. I already looked into it. Everyone is driving through a border crossing twenty minutes south of you. I already found you a ride, paid your expenses, and bought you a ticket. You can't say no. They'll pick you up tomorrow at 10 a.m. You need this. Love you."

I hadn't been active in recovery community the entire time I had been in Arizona. There was one meeting in Patagonia, but the closest person in age to me was fifty years older and there was more talk about cancer than being of service to the new man. It also met on Friday at seven during our Shabbat celebration. I had only attended once.

I was a little scared to face the friends I'd made from around the world who would be at this conference. I felt like such a mess. I had gone from being the picture of success to feeling lost and confused. But the conference did feel like exactly what the doctor ordered so I arranged the time off and packed my bags.

The drive down was a breath of fresh air. We laughed and cried and talked about God, ourselves, and recovery the whole time. When I got down to the conference, though, I started seeing all the people I knew, hundreds of them, and I started feeling really out of place. It was New Year's Eve and everyone I knew was in a festive mood. I was introspective, thinking about the whirlwind of a year that was ending, and a little nervous about the year that was about to start. The clock counted down, the fireworks went off, and everyone exchanged warm hugs, smiles, and greetings of "Happy New Year," but I felt like an outsider looking in.

I walked over to the dance hoping to at least distract myself, but the DJ was terrible, so I walked outside. I found a young guy there smoking and we started talking. Neither of us was feeling the dance, so we decided to walk over to the "marathon meeting." (Frequently at recovery conferences there will be meetings that happen around the clock. They start every hour on the hour and have rotating speakers and leaders.) When we showed up, there were two guys sitting in the audience—an older gentleman who looked to be in his fifties and one in his early twenties—but no speaker and no leader.

The older man asked, "Are you guys here to lead the meeting?"

"Uh . . . no," I said. 'We just came here for a meeting."

"Well, how long have you got sober?"

"Nine years," I said.

"Ninety days," said my companion.

"Nine years, why don't you speak, and ninety days, why don't you lead?" the man suggested. "There's a format on the table. Let's get this show on the road!"

It was honestly the last thing I wanted to do, but I agreed.

In recovery, you describe your experience coming out of addiction, the strength you've found in faith, and the hope for the future you've found in your relationship with God. As I started to share my story, memories started flooding my mind. I remembered all the miracles that God had worked in my life. The moment in the bathroom when I said "God help me" and he took the obsession to drink and use away. All the people He had put in my path that had done or said exactly the right thing at exactly the right moment. Even my friend from Canada who had arranged for me to be at the conference when I needed it most. In moments where I couldn't see the road in front of me, every time I had stepped out in faith, I found Him there. Sharing what God had done in my life with a room of complete strangers actually started renewing my faith that even in this moment, God had a plan.

After the meeting, the twenty-something guy who had been standing with the older gentleman at the start of the meeting came and introduced himself to me. His name was Zach. He said he had been feeling just as disconnected as I had when I showed up at the conference, but something I had said in my talk gave him hope. We stayed up all night talking and laughing. As the hours rolled by, I realized that this was what I'd been missing—and what I was built for. God had given me new life, built from the rubble of my former existence. He gave me a story, a testimony—not just for myself, but for others.

I knew I had to leave Arizona. I called Christine the next day and asked if the offer to live and work with them was still on the table. It was. I knew I wasn't running away, but running towards. I had a purpose. I didn't know yet exactly how it would play out, but I knew I had to go back to San Diego.

The Power to Change

CHAPTER 6:
Pride & Prejudice

Leaving Tree of Life was much easier than I thought. I was honest with everyone about my decision and its reasons, and they respected it. I boxed up my stuff, we rented a trailer, and Christine's husband Roberto and I moved my stuff back to San Diego, just three weeks after I had moved it to Arizona.

Arriving back in San Diego was more excitement than culture shock. I was blessed with a beautiful little guest house, a car to drive when I needed it, and a small stipend for food and living necessities. It was perfect. I was being creative and of service to others. I was reconnecting with friends in a much more humble and honest way than I ever had before.

A week after I got back to San Diego, I was hanging out with Patrick, a guy I used to mentor in recovery. At one point in our conversation, he asked me, "What are you doing with the 11th Step?"

I assumed that he was imagining I'd have some deep insight on the subject, having just returned home from a "spiritual community." "Well", I replied, "When I was out in Arizona we had sunrise and sunset fire ceremonies, Kirtan on Wednesday, Shabbat on Friday, Havdalah on Saturday, and a Lakota Sioux Sweat Lodge on every new moon."

He looked at me as if I'd just grown horns. "What the hell is all that?"

"You just asked me what I did for Step 11."

"Yeah, not all that. What do you in the morning and at night? When you wake up, do you pray, ask God to direct your thinking, review your plans for the day, and meditate with a spiritual book? Before you go to bed, do you look at how well you did during the day, make a list of any amends you need to make, that stuff? A.A.? Step 11?"

"Oh, that. I used to do that when I was newly sober, but you know, like they say, 'What used to be the hunch or the occasional inspiration gradually becomes a working part of the mind.'"

"Hmm . . ." he replied. "How's that workin' for ya?"

I was pissed. But how could I respond when I knew it wasn't working? It had worked great when I had done it, and in that moment, I realized that I'd been sharing at meetings for seven years and acting as if the experiences I had in my first two years were still happening.

"What are you doing for Step 11, Patrick?"

"Just that—prayer and meditation in the morning, carrying God's plan for my day with me and reviewing how well I did at night, and taking that inventory into the next day to try to be a little bit better tomorrow than I was today."

"And how's that working for you?"

"Amazing. I've never felt more directed or had so much peace my whole life."

"When did you start?"

"My sponsor Brian and I started listening to this guy from Texas, Mark Houston. Never heard anyone talk about recovery like him. I actually brought you the workshop we listen to on CD. Thought you'd like it. It's six CDs. Here."

He handed me the CDs. I knew I needed something for Step 11, but I didn't want to commit to listening to them. "Thanks, Pat. You know I'm super busy right now, so I don't know when I'll get a chance to listen, but I really appreciate it."

The truth was that I had all the time in the world, but I was so convinced that there was something wrong with me that the 12 Steps wouldn't fix. I secretly believed that I needed a lot of medication and a really good psychiatrist, and wondered if I'd be better off in a nuthouse.

Later, figuring that it couldn't hurt, I put the first CD in and started listening. I had never heard anything like it in my life. Mark explained alcoholism as a three-part disease of body (physical craving), mind (mental obsession), and spirit (spiritual malady—restless, irritable, discontent). He described how, at ten years sober, he lost his marriage and his career and ended up in a psych ward in Texas, where a friend eventually reached him with the message of recovery. He explained that the internal spiritual malady can only be arrested, never cured, and that if someone has been treating it with liquor and drugs, when they get sober and don't treat it with a powerful, foundational relationship with God, it frequently shows up in other areas.

He was reading my mail! I had this spiritual malady bad, and it was showing up in a ton of areas—sex addiction, an eating disorder, anxiety, compulsive spending, compulsive exercise . . . I could probably name twenty more areas if I really thought about it. All of this had shown up for Mark up at ten years sober—I was just a few months shy of that milestone.

I listened to all six CDs that night. At the end of one of the sessions, there were questions and answers, and he gave someone who asked a question his email address. It was an AOL email limited to ten characters, so he was one character short of his name. I thought that if those CDs were over ten years old, there was no way he still had the same email, but it was my one hope of getting a hold of the guy, so I gave it a shot. I had never heard such a clear message of hope before from one who clearly knew what it was like to live in my skin. Taking the one-in-a-million chance he would receive the message, I poured my heart out in an email, figuring this might be my one opportunity to talk to someone who actually understood me. When I pressed "Send" and went to bed, it was past five in the morning.

Later that morning, I woke up and checked my email. Mark had written me back, and said it just so happened he was going to be in San Diego that coming weekend. He also explained that he only mentored six guys at a time, but the night before, he had just let one mentee go who wouldn't work with him, so he had an opening. He wasn't going to make any promises, but he gave me an assignment to inventory areas of current unmanageability in my life, and he gave me his number so we could coordinate meeting that weekend.

The exercise he gave me had questions like:

"Are you in control of your negative emotions or are they in control of you?"

"When asked about how you are doing, do you say that you are doing well? Even though you say that, do you often know deep down that this is not the truth?"

"Do you want to enjoy a certain reputation, but know in your heart that you don't deserve it?"

"In a conversation, do you actually listen, or just impatiently wait for your turn to talk?"

There were dozens of tough questions that made me uncomfortable, but as I continued to push on and did my best to answer them honestly, I got the strange sensation that this was the beginning of a road to true freedom.

When I met with Mark, he started by asking me questions about AA's 12 Steps.

"No matter what process you're starting, if you start with an answer, you'll end up with the same answer you started with," he told me. "So let's begin this process with a question, and the most appropriate questions to ask right now would be, 'Am I an alcoholic? Am I an addict? Am I both? Am I neither?'"

It had been almost ten years since I had asked those questions of myself, and honestly, they terrified me. I secretly worried that there was more wrong with me than that.

Mark took me through AA's "Big Book," turning each of the statements it made about alcoholism into questions. In the process, I realized I had treated all my normal human problems with alcohol and drugs, and in sobriety I had turned to other things to treat those same problems—people, sex, money, work, control, exercise, diet, and more. Instead of turning to God, I had taken my internally unmanageable emotional state and tried to treat it externally.

Even my spiritual "seeking" had been done in a way that bolstered my pride through self-knowledge, not surrender to God. Mark really challenged me on what he called my "intellectual agnosticism and spiritual pride." Why was I so open to Eastern philosophy, and so closed off to Western faith? Was it because I had hope that I could overcome the world on my own power, whereas faith actually required the power of God?

Then he asked me, "How's that workin' for ya?"

We both knew the answer.

Mark went on. "You tell a tree by its fruit, right? A lemon tree looks like an orange tree or a grapefruit tree, but a lemon tree never produces grapefruit, right?"

"Right."

"So, since you're seeking, why don't you look at the fruit of the 'spiritual' people in your life and see if you find any patterns in those people's lives."

I knew several people who claimed various faiths. I looked at their lives for criteria that I deemed to be the "good fruit" of successful living—stability and consistency, successful friendships and romantic relationships, joy, lack of unresolved conflict, good reports about them from others, and how I felt when I was around them.

The results I found were surprising. Many of the people I knew who claimed to be Buddhist or New Age walked away from difficult situations or conflict rather than dealing with them head-on. They'd engage when it benefited them, but detach at the first sign of conflict. Most of them had a trail of broken relationships and unfinished business. Most seemed to be always seeking but never finding (myself included).

Most of my Jewish friends, though not all, were Jewish by birth, but far from practice. Some had gone full-bore religious Hasidic, but they seemed to be more concerned with the letter of the law, strict kosher, and religious dress than a relationship with G-d. This was true of my Muslim friends, too. You could recognize them by how they dressed, but the way they lived didn't result in healthy, consistent relationships. I thought that some of that might be cultural misunderstanding too, so I didn't want to judge too much. The westerners I knew who had converted, I noticed, became increasingly distant from their friends and family.

I also knew a handful of Hindus. One, my friend Thomas, had done an invocation to one of their gods, Kali, and died violently a week later. Most of the ones I knew, however, were really gentle people who believed in karma as a ruling force in the universe—that if you did good, you received good, that if you did evil you received evil in return, and that life was essentially about being good to overcome past evils from former lifetimes. In a similar vein, a couple of people I knew practiced Jainism and wouldn't eat anything except fallen fruit, so as to not cause pain to any living thing, including trees. I respected their devotion, as I too had tried to live a life where I didn't cause suffering, though no matter how hard I tried, I failed.

I discovered something unexpected when I inventoried my Christian friends. There were, of course, some who claimed Christ, but lived counter to what they claimed to believe. But there were others who really lived what they claimed to believe, and their lives were amazing. Though I had judged them for being small-minded, when I looked at their lives I saw really good fruit.

One of those was my friend Jeremy, a young man I used to mentor in recovery. It drove me crazy that he was Christian. I kept trying to get him to read non-Christian books about the life of Christ that viewed Christ as a prophet or enlightened man, but not as God in the flesh. My goal was to "broaden his mind." I bought him The Gospel According to Jesus by Stephen Mitchell, a book that puts forth the (unsubstantiated) claim that Christ was the bastard child of Mary and a Roman guard, and that He, like the Buddha, overcame the world and his impossible situation on his own power, becoming enlightened and teaching from that place of personal enlightenment. I gave Jeremy that book as a gift on the occasion of the celebration of his ninety days sober. He politely refused the gift, saying that between the Bible and AA's "Big Book," he had as much as he could handle for the next year. I suggested that he put down the Bible and read this instead. He said he'd already committed to reading the Bible in a year. So I waited.

On his one-year-sober anniversary, I offered the book again. This time, Jeremy said, "Hey man, listen. I know that you're not Christian, and that you want me to see things like you do, but I don't. My faith is the foundation of my life. Everything I do, everything I see, is founded in my faith. I don't expect you to see things the way I do, but I expect you to respect me and not try to change me, especially in this area that is foundational to who I am . . . and it's clear to me that you don't respect me enough to let me have my faith. Thank you for giving me so much this year, but I need to find another mentor."

To me, that was the nail in the coffin for Jeremy. He was so closed-minded. The nerve—refusing my gift and then throwing it in my face like that! I literally could not see the truth of what he was saying. I was so caught up in the idea that I was right and that he was a fool. Now, five years later, I was reconsidering.

In contrast to my downward spiral of destruction and disillusionment, Jeremy had gotten married, built a successful business, and miraculous circumstances seemed to follow him wherever he went. When I had a party, I always invited him and his wife, and without fail, several of my non-Christian friends would come up to me afterwards and say things like, "Who were they?"

"They were so nice."

"Could I get their number?"

"Are they going to be at your next party?"

Every single time. There was something so attractive and magnetic about who they were that people always asked about them—in fact, they were the only guests of mine people ever asked about.

Mark suggested that, after looking at the fruit of my spiritual and religious friends, I should determine who had the best fruit and talk to them about their faith. (He later told me that I had so much spiritual prejudice and intellectual pride, that looking at evidence in my life and in the lives of my friends was the only thing he thought that might shatter some of my tidy arguments and justifications around what I'd believed.)

I called Jeremy and asked him if I could go to church with him and his wife. I'm so grateful he didn't make a big deal about it. So many of the Christians I had known growing up had been so over-zealous about getting me to a Christian event that they were either unattractively pushy or somewhat dishonest. There had been several times I had been invited to join a barbecue with "some cool people hanging out on the beach" or come hear "some great bands," only to discover that the people at the event were all Christian, the bands only played songs about Jesus, and inevitably, someone would get up and share a testimony or preach about how I needed to repent and get "saved." I called it "the Christian bait-and-switch," and it was so offensive to me. It seemed to me that all the Christians I knew judged me and wanted to change me. But Jeremy wasn't like that. He just said, "Sure. We go to a seven o'clock evening service, and we usually go to dinner after. You're welcome to meet us there." He was cool, and let me find my own way. He made me feel welcome, but didn't make the situation awkward.

I met them at church that Sunday. Jeremy and his wife introduced me to their friends and saved me a seat so that we could sit together. The pastor was funny and relatable and he laid out the Gospel message in a way that I had never heard before.

I thought that Christians believed you had to be good in order to be accepted by God. The pastor explained that this idea was the problem with religion and religious philosophies—that we couldn't make ourselves perfect on our own power. Christianity wasn't about that at all. It was about accepting an invitation to know God as a loving Father who matures us in His time and by His power, in the context of a loving relationship, like a father to his child.

I was shocked. There wasn't a single thing preached that I had a problem with. I had somehow expected fire and brimstone, and what I got was love and acceptance. I thought, If God wants a relationship with me, this is the only way it could work. If it was up to me to make myself perfect, to burn though karma, to live a perfect life, I'd never measure up. But if it wasn't that at all, that could work.

The pastor asked if anyone wanted a relationship like that with God. I raised my hand. I was still on the fence about the Virgin Birth, the Resurrection, and creation versus evolution, but I decided to give church a try and started going every Sunday.

CHAPTER 7:
Power Tools

As I continued through AA's 12 Steps with Mark, they started to make sense to me in a very different way. I thought I had understood Step 1. At nineteen, I had admitted I was powerless over alcohol and my life had become unmanageable. But now, at twenty-nine, I looked at it from a completely different perspective.

When I was nineteen, I had great hope in so many things. I thought that when I got into the right school . . . won the awards . . . got the job, girl, car, or house . . . got in good shape . . . had so much money—then my shoulders would drop, my skin would fit right, and I would feel like life made sense. Now, I had achieved all those things. They were my best attempts at creating a happy and successful life, and they all failed. It wasn't that any of them were bad. I just saw that they couldn't be the foundation I was banking on to build a stable and joy-filled life.

I lived with so much tension between my inner and outer worlds, and I had always tried to fix it or distract myself from it in a self-destructive way. It was a self-perpetuating cycle. When I felt restless, irritable, and unhappy with some aspect of my life, rather than dealing with the situation head-on (which always felt too overwhelming), I would spend money I didn't have to impress people I didn't like—and later resent them for it. Or I'd sleep with someone I didn't really know or care about, experience a huge rush, and immediately be filled with painful guilt. I was always searching, never satisfied. In my drinking days, I turned to drugs and alcohol to mask those feelings, and in sobriety I turned to other things that were every bit as destructive, if not more so. In my own power, I had seemingly no ability to change these patterns. That's Step 1, and I had it bad.

My attention in Step 1 had always been on the physical and mental, and my position in recovery was all about staying away from bad things, not going towards good things. All this had done was keep me in a perpetual game of whack-a-mole with my sins. If I wasn't in full-blown drug addiction or alcoholism, I was indulging a sex addiction or compulsive spending. When I was trying to get spending under "control," I became neurotic about my physical health, exercising in an extreme way to try to overcome body image issues, or developing an unhealthy obsession with healthy eating until it became a neurosis called orthorexia.

I began to realize that an emotional and spiritual sickness—a restlessness, irritability, sense of impending doom, and fear of intimacy—had always been the underlying driver of all those destructive behaviors. This was the legitimate problem to which I had continually responded with these illegitimate solutions, trying to find relief. No matter how hard I tried on my own power to change my internal condition, I had failed, and the more I tried, the more painful my failure became. To the core of my being, I knew I needed to know and rely on God in a far deeper way than I ever had before. God had to be real, and had to have the power to change my life.

I had never believed in a devil, but I could see through my own experience that no matter how many people were around me, championing and cheering me on, I had a little voice in my head speaking against me. No matter what I accomplished, it never felt like enough. I continually heard these thoughts:

They don't know you. If they did, they wouldn't be cheering you on. They'd hate you and be disgusted with you.

You're a fraud. You're going to fail, and when you fail everyone around you is going to laugh at you.

You're too broken ever to find real love. The things you've done, and the things you've allowed to be done to you, have disqualified you from all that.

Mark told me that the name Satan means "accuser." I never knew that before. I thought of pitchforks, horns, and fire, not whispers, accusations, and condemnation. When I learned this, I started to look at my personal battles completely differently. I had always seen them as being my own, and that I had to fight alone. I had gotten into the Buddhist idea of inter-being—that all things are connected, and that our spiritual task is to find harmony and transcend suffering by overcoming all internal attachments. But all that approach had produced for me was a feeling of disconnection from everything, not more connection. Now my newfound faith was telling me that I had a real enemy who was actively working to keep me disconnected from God, myself, and others. Even though that concept had seemed crazy to me before, now I found that my experience kept lining up with what I was being taught. For instance, I learned that the accuser will attack your identity relentlessly, saying you're something other than who God says you are, until you believe him. When you finally agree with the lies he's telling you and start to live differently than the way God wants you to, in some ways it becomes easier because the accusations stop. The enemy doesn't need to accuse you anymore he has stolen the vision God has for your life. If you tried to break free of the lies and realign your beliefs with the truth, however, he will ramp up the accusations again, trying to keep you in bondage.

The voice of the accuser had led me to believe so many negative things about myself. Yet I had also been aware of another voice, one that told me not to believe those accusations, but to trust the greatness I secretly believed lay dormant inside me. I didn't know how to tap into that voice, but somehow, I knew deep down that it was there.

Now, Mark was helping me to realize that one of the things that might have stifled that little voice cheering me on was my own intellectualism. I had read a ton of books full of ideas. Some were full of truth, but now I was beginning to see that even truth, if it's read but never applied, is only synthetic knowledge. In Christianity, everything is turned upside down to an intellectual, because knowledge and transformation happen relationally, not intellectually. God is a person, not a set of principles. I come to know Him and experience His presence in the context of relationship. It isn't about doing out of knowing, but knowing out of the experience of doing—walking by faith, not by sight. If I already know, or think I know, I don't need faith. And what I found is that if I think I know, it is likely to prevent me from doing, rather than launching me into doing. Intellectual pride is a funny thing.

Mark gave me this prayer to use: "God please enable me to set aside everything I think I know for an open mind and a new experience." So simple, but so powerful.

As I asked God to empty me out so that He could fill me up properly, I began to become aware of just how empty I really was. It started to dawn on me that so far, the only result I had gained from the Steps was self-knowledge . . . which couldn't help me. I had experienced many profound realizations through the Steps, but without the power of God moving and transforming me through this process, this self-knowledge alone did not produce change. When I was nineteen, I was full of hope that knowing myself better would empower me to act differently. At twenty-nine, I had burnt through all that hope. I had done all the things I thought would lead to happiness and fulfillment, and they had left me bankrupt and heartbroken. I became convinced that no matter how much I knew, without God, I had no power to change.

In the absence of a real relationship with God, I had based my entire life and identity around faulty dependence on people and stories I'd made up about myself. I was constantly trying to prove why others were wrong and I was right so I didn't have to face the reality that I had no idea who I was, that the image and identity I was trying to portray were flimsy, and that I was fragile and weak. But as I began to build a genuine connection with God, I found that, for the first time, I could look deep into my hurt, shame, anger, and other areas I had never dared to look at before. In the process, every excuse I had used for years to avoid God—my pride, preconceived ideas, and even my experience living before I knew Him—began to slip away. Instead, I became convinced that no matter what I found, God loved me and had already forgiven me, and no matter how hard it got, He'd carry me through it.

The first thing God helped me realize was that every obsession I'd ever had was the result of an identity crisis. Whenever I tried to get my identity from anything outside of Him, I ended up scrambling for power that wasn't there. The more it eluded me, the more obsessively I pursued it in whatever I was trying to identify myself with.

When I found my identity in being a raw food vegan, having what was, in my mind, the "healthiest diet on the planet," it wasn't healthy—I was obsessed. I refused to eat anything that wasn't raw, vegan, and organic. If I couldn't find anything that fit that criteria, I would just starve. Then I'd get "hangry" and out of my mind. But of course, it wouldn't be my fault for being a crazy, obsessed, self-identified vegan—it would be somebody else's fault for not having choices that pandered to my crazy diet. I had to make other people wrong to make my life choices make sense. I was 6'3" and weighed 145 pounds. My hair was falling out. Everyone told me I didn't look healthy, but I couldn't see it. They were all wrong. I was obsessed with being right about being a raw-food vegan. It gave me a feeling of control and a feeling of being better than everyone around me.

I did the same thing with sex addiction. When I was lonely, I needed somebody to take care of my loneliness, because I couldn't stand to be alone with myself. I would obsess about it, act out, then regret what I'd done. When the obsession had its hooks in me, though, I didn't feel like I could help myself.

The Power to Change

For so many years, I had been caught in a hopeless catch-22—trying to play God and live as though He didn't exist, grabbing for power and control in different identities and lifestyles, falling short constantly, and then blaming others and obsessively trying to prove them wrong and myself right. The resentments I carried toward God, others, and even myself were all obsessions—re-sentiment, obsessive thought. Yet I could never see the hypocrisy and insanity in what I was doing, in how I was living.

Now I was starting to see the ugly reality, but for the first time, I had hope, because I had God. I remembered a quote from St. Francis of Assisi: "Wear the world like a loose garment." I can only do that when my identity isn't found in my activity and performance. When my identity is secure in my relationship with God, I can wear my activities loosely—put them on, take them off, no big deal. But when I find my identity in what I'm doing, or in how others see or feel about me, I wear the world like a suit of armor. To be okay, I need people to recognize me for what I'm trying to be. When they don't, I get resentful and must prove them wrong so I don't have to look at myself. All of that causes incredible dis-ease. I am constantly out of sorts, and my relationships are always out of sorts as well.

I came to accept that I am either in the Spirit—that is, letting God be God in my life—or in obsession, where I am trying to play God in my life. The latter only creates internal unmanageability, which produces external unmanageability.

Again, strangely I felt hope as I digested these hard and ugly truths about myself. I was beginning to trust not only that I was going to be all right, but that on the other side of letting this truth do its work in me, God was going to set me on a solid ground my feet had never known. The truth was going to set me free.

Mark had me write what in recovery terms is known as Step 4, a searching and fearless moral inventory of myself. I inventoried my resentments—the people I was unwilling or unable to forgive. I inventoried my fear. I inventoried my sexual misconduct and all the take-it-to-the-grave secrets I had been hiding. I got them all down on paper with Mark's direction, and then I looked at them.

This process of looking at my resentments had two parts. First, I looked at what the person had done and how it affected my self-esteem, pride, ambitions, security, relationships (both friendships and romantic), and finances. Even though I could see intellectually that I should have been relying on God rather than people, and that I'd hijacked my own happiness by demanding people treat me perfectly¬, that realization didn't get me any closer to being able to let the resentments go, especially when I had really been harmed.

Mark asked me to go back through each resentment and ask myself honestly if I had ever done, even in spirit, the things I resented those people for doing to me—to them or to anyone else, ever. Then he asked me to put it all down on paper.

There was one resentment I didn't think I was able to forgive. I had taken a guy in the recovery fellowship named Nick under my wing when he was newly sober. I considered him a friend. When he wanted to pursue my ex-girlfriend, he spread vicious rumors about me to her, her friends, and her acquaintances, trying to undermine my character. He attacked my character, integrity, and sincerity in helping others, painting me as a predator. Ninety-five percent of the rumors he spread were complete fabrications, but there was one that was actually true. It wasn't true in the way he was painting it, but it had an element of truth I had unintentionally kept from my ex, though it would seem intentional now if it ever came to light.

Never had I been so specifically targeted in such a terrible way, and by one I had intentionally tried to make feel included. I had gone on the attack, directly confronting and discrediting Nick in front of my ex, then his friends, and then those with whom he had influence. I went from including him to going out of my way to make him feel unwelcome at social gatherings. I even went so far as to dress up as a caricature of him at a 5,000-person recovery Halloween dance, intentionally making him look foolish in front of our community.

I wanted to be seen as the perfect boyfriend and for people to believe that the breakup with my ex was her fault, not mine. I wanted to be seen as a shining example of recovery and a great and selfless person. But I was afraid I wasn't as good as all that, and if I didn't discredit Nick first, I would be exposed, abandoned, and alone. I really believed I'd only be loved if I was perfect, and if people believed him, they'd reject me. In holding on to this resentment, I had effectively turned my whole sense of who I was over to him. He had to treat me right in order for me to be okay.

Despite seeing these truths about my insecurities, my heart still held on to the hurt of that betrayal. It didn't feel good holding this unforgiveness in my heart, but I didn't know how to release it. I had been wronged, and no matter how hard I tried to forgive him, I couldn't on my own, partly because I believed that forgiveness included agreeing that what Nick did to me was okay when it wasn't.

Mark again challenged me to look back at my own life to see if I had ever done, even in spirit, the things I resented Nick for doing to me. I resented Nick because he tried to sleep with my ex-girlfriend. He lied about me and tried to destroy my reputation in the recovery community. He would grandstand while sharing at recovery meetings and claim he had finished the 12 Steps, though he had never made amends to me. Basically, I believed he didn't respect me or what was mine and was out to destroy me.

Well, as hard as it was to admit, I looked at my own life and saw that I had slept with ex-girlfriends of my friends. I had gossiped about others, focusing on their flaws to try to influence others and improve my own position—I had done this with Nick in this very situation. I had also tried to pretend everything was okay when it wasn't to make myself look like a great example of recovery at meetings—not just so I could help others, but so I would be envied. Wow.

That admission leveled the playing field. I suddenly had no position from which to look down on Nick. I saw him as my brother. I saw that we both badly needed God. And the moment I saw him like this, not only was I able to I forgive him—I also saw places where I needed to ask his forgiveness, and the forgiveness of those in our community whose lives I'd polluted with all this drama.

Mark told me I was to look for my mistakes and be willing to clean up whatever part of the situation was my fault, even if it was only five or ten percent. I was willing. I really wanted to be free. My part to clean up, as far as I knew, was the way I had iced Nick out of recovery parties and activities and gossiped about him at my group, other groups, and to the men he mentored. There was also my attempt to publicly humiliate him at the Halloween party, and my sharing of confidential information about him I had learned from an ex of his to further destroy his character in the eyes of others. I now saw that I had harmed Nick with these actions. I had undermined his ability to be helpful to others and harmed the new men in our groups by gossiping to them about Nick. I had also harmed our group and its members by creating division rather than unity, putting my right to be offended above the wellbeing of the group and the new members who were looking for help with their addictions.

I had even wished that Nick would relapse so I wouldn't have to deal with him anymore . . . and he had, before I had my change of heart. But now my heart was broken for him. I began trying to find out where he was. I also made amends to everyone else I had harmed in our group. The most amazing result came from that—I found that people respected me more after I took responsibility for my actions than they had before there was even a problem.

A few months later, I was standing out front of a meeting when Nick walked up. It was his first meeting back after a relapse that nearly killed him, and as God would have it, I was the first person he saw because I had stepped out of the meeting to take a work call. I credit God with His perfect timing.

Nick walked straight up to me and gave me a huge hug. "Morgan, it's so good to see you," he said sincerely. "You're a sight for sore eyes."

"Nick, I can't even tell you," I said, stunned. "I've been praying for you, and am so happy to see you here alive!" Without hesitation, I seized the moment. "Listen, do you have a second? I owe you a pretty serious amends."

"You owe me an amends? After all I did to you? Are you kidding?"

"No, I'm dead serious," I insisted. "I've been working with an amazing sponsor and when I went through inventory, I saw all of the stuff that I did, and it was ugly. Can we talk about it?"

Nick smiled, and said, "Sure. Man, it's good to see you."

We talked for most of the rest of the meeting. I owned all the ugliness of what I had done. At the end of our conversation, Nick asked me to mentor him through the same process I was going through with Mark[1].

Through this journey of forgiving Nick, I found it to be a principle that whenever there is someone I don't think I can forgive, looking for common ground in seeing where I have acted like them will free me from the tyranny of unforgiveness and show me a path forward.

Going through Steps 4-9 of the 12 Steps—confession, contrition, and change, which essentially are Christian repentance—I started to understand why Christ said so often, "I have not come to call the righteous, but sinners, to repentance.[2]" There is something that happens in me when I am able, without reservation, to confess to God where I have fallen short. Seeing the destructive results of my own handiwork breaks my heart, and when I can cry out to God with a genuinely broken heart, He not only takes away the hurt—He also changes my heart in a way that only He can, so that I know Him and my fellow man better through it. The purpose of the 12 Steps isn't to complete them 1-12, but to practice a lifestyle of knowing and relying on God, and the doorway to that is a lifestyle of

---

[1] Over the next several years, we became good friends. Nick came to know Jesus and also battled brain cancer—I got to be around for both. He has been and continues to be a great teacher and a great friend. I love him, and am so grateful for all we've been through.

[2] See Matthew 9:13, Mark 2:17, Luke 5:32.

repentance—admitting fault, growing through that, and letting God mature me as I practiced.

I had created a lot of chaos and a lot of harm living sober without God, and it took almost two years to track down all the people to whom I owed amends. Girls, friends, employers, people from meetings—there were over a hundred people and institutions on that list. Some amends were fairly minor, while others were really major. There was a marked difference between these amends and every other apology I had ever made, because God was at the center of them. I knew that He had already forgiven me eternally, so it wasn't about convincing anyone to accept my apology. Rather, I was there to frankly admit my wrongs and do anything in my power to right them, no matter the personal cost. Instead of making a groveling apology and talking about God, I let the other person ask questions and respond however they wanted to, and let my actions be evidence of my faith.

I made the final two amends on December 31, 2006 at about ten in the evening, just before ringing in the new year. The last amends I made was to a young man named Alex. He had looked up to me in recovery and I had let him down badly—so badly, in fact, that his resentment towards me had led him back to alcohol, and he had almost drunk himself to death. It broke my heart to hear how badly my carelessness had harmed someone I truly cared for. I left our meeting not knowing if our friendship would ever be repaired to where it had been before, but knowing that I had done everything in my power to make that possible, and in doing that, both of us had become free that night. It was an amazing feeling to walk out of that room knowing that I didn't owe anyone anything anymore, and that there was absolutely nothing anyone could find out about me that someone else didn't already know. No more secrets, no more debt. That's freedom.

The Power to Change

CHAPTER 8:
Miracle Grow

Over the next three years, I grew in my relationship with God and continued to serve others out of my newfound experience with Him through the 12 Steps. I only went to church occasionally, as I was living in Vancouver and couldn't find a church I really connected with there. But I did meet some Christians who became good friends, and I really tried to live a spiritual life.

At this point, I had accepted Christ, but there was plenty of growth that needed to happen. I had never really read the Bible, and was still on the fence about the Virgin Birth, Resurrection, and creationism vs. evolution. I thought purity until marriage was an outdated ideal. However, God was working things out.

Through the Steps, I had developed a sexual ideal—a vision for my future romantic relationships. I had learned a lot from inventorying my past and I didn't want to repeat the same mistakes, so I looked at all the things I did wrong and made a list of things that I wanted to do instead in the future:

1. Instead of having sex first and developing a relationship after, I will only have physical intimacy after emotional intimacy is established.

2. Instead of just looking at outer beauty, I will only pursue a girl I also find mentally and emotionally stimulating.

3. We need to be able to laugh together.

4. She has to have healthy friendships with women.

5. We need to have a shared interest in growing spiritually.

6. We need to share a healthy, active lifestyle.

7. We will have honest, open, proactive (not reactionary) conversations.

8. We must have shared interests.

9. We must get along with each other's friends.

10. We must have a heart for service.

In late 2007, I met a girl who I thought fulfilled all those conditions. We met through one of my best friends, who was also one of her best friends, so I knew that we would get along well in our community of friends. She was involved in a 12-Step fellowship for family members of alcoholics and addicts. We met at a movie where we ended up having an impromptu popcorn fight with each other. I thought it was a match made in heaven . . . and I was scared to death.

I called Mark and asked what to do. He asked if I would consider not sleeping with her for ninety days. I agreed to wait until the seventh date and talk to her about it.

"I've done it wrong in the past and I want to do this differently," I explained to her. "I really want to get to know you before we take that step. I want to build emotional intimacy with you before physical intimacy is on the table for discussion."

I thought she would think I was a weirdo, but surprisingly, she was so touched that I was willing to wait for her. We waited exactly ninety days. The night we slept together for the first time, I was so sure it would be completely different than any of the relationships I had before. But it wasn't. Sure, we had gotten to know each other a bit, but we were still in the honeymoon phase and on our best behavior. We were in a "committed" relationship, whatever that means, but there wasn't a real legal commitment to each other. Once we started sleeping together, that old addiction to emotional and physical validation kicked in and the relationship started the familiar downward spiral to not working out.

I had really thought that this girl was "the one," and that getting to know her a little would be enough, but it wasn't. I still had plenty to work through with God. I hadn't yet figured out that almost daily pornography use wasn't healthy. No matter how much I wanted a healthy relationship, without God and His Word, it was going to be beyond my grasp.

In spring of 2010, I moved back to San Diego and got involved in serving and mentoring in recovery there. One of the men I started mentoring was a guy named Steve. We had a ton in common, and though I was more mature in my recovery, he was far more mature in his faith.

That Easter, I asked Steve if I could join him at his church. Steve went to a mega-church that sat 3,500 people a service, and since Easter is essentially the Super Bowl of the Christian calendar year, the service was totally packed out. We ended up sitting with a bunch of people from a young Christian recovery group about forty rows back from the stage.

There was nothing about the service that appealed to me. First of all, I hate sitting in the back, because I get distracted. To make matters worse, the people to my right and left were talking through the service, the worship music was performed by a contemporary gospel choir and I didn't know any of the songs, and it was Easter—I already knew the story.

At the end of the service, there was an altar call. Hundreds of people came forward. Though I didn't feel especially close to God, I also didn't think I needed to go recommit. I had already been in that back room once—someone had prayed for me and given me a free Bible. I was good on that.

After the altar call, however, they invited the remaining congregation to join in communion. I considered myself Christian, so I figured I'd partake. When the pastor started praying for the communion, something very different started happening with me. The only way I can describe it that God started speaking to me. It wasn't audible, but suddenly there were thoughts in my mind that had never been there before, and they challenged everything I had believed about, well, the nature of everything. They had nothing to do with the service or the communion message, but they did have to do with my faith. The way I believe God spoke to me that day was really similar, I'd come to find out, to the way God spoke to Job in the whirlwind.[3]

"So . . . you love Carl Sagan, the Discovery Channel, and National Geographic. You love astronomy and science. You have never doubted what Carl Sagan has said about your galaxy and its place in the universe. In fact, you believe that in your little tiny galaxy there are between 350 and 500 billion stars, and if you counted them, one per second, it would take between 3,000 and 4,000 years. You also believe that in the known universe there are more galaxies than there are stars in your galaxy, that most of those galaxies are many times the size of the Milky Way, and that if all humankind had done since the dawn of man was count stars, you would have barely scratched the surface of all the stars that are there. You also believe that I created the universe—that it didn't originate in a vacuum or in some alternate universe. You believe that I'm big enough to create that, yet somehow doubt My ability to knock up a virgin or raise a dead guy? Really?"

"Okay," I thought. "Fine, I'll give that to You. But what about dinosaurs? What about evolution?"

"What about evolution?" He replied. "You used to love dinosaurs when you were a kid. You made your dad take you to the Denver Natural History Museum to see the bones. In fact, I bet you know how many fully intact dinosaur skeletons archaeologists have found."

---

[3] *See Job, chapters 38-42.*

"You're right." Strange Jeopardy factoid. "I do. About 10,000."

"10,000 fully intact dinosaur fossils that are supposedly tens to hundreds of millions years old—but in the whole history of archeology, they've failed to find a single skeletal remain that conclusively links man to ape. Do you think that's at all weird?"

"Wow. Yes, I admitted. Since You put it that way, it's actually very weird."

"So do you think it's possible that you don't know everything?"

"Yes. Actually, I think it's probable that I don't know much."

Almost as soon as I had that thought, the prayer for communion ended and we took communion as a church. As I ate the communion wafer and drank the juice, God revealed Christ's sacrifice to me in a way that broke my heart, and suddenly everything I thought I knew shifted. It suddenly became really important to get baptized and be discipled. Though I didn't know what either meant, I knew I needed both.

Steve looked over and saw me with the empty communion cup in my hand, tears streaming down my face. "You okay?" he asked.

"Yeah," I said. "Better than okay. I need to get baptized."

Steve explained that baptism was "just an outward expression of an inward change." He made it sound like a religious ceremony, but I knew there had to be more to it. The church offered baptisms once a quarter, but something in me felt like that wasn't the right call. There would have been a point in my life where I would have shown up dressed all in white at the front of the line, but something about that approach seemed foreign to me now. There was something happening in me that I couldn't explain, something far too precious and personal to carelessly put on display. When I learned that the church's discipleship school was also doing baptisms the same day as the corporate church baptisms, but that it would just be a small, private ceremony and not a big show, I signed up. That sounded perfect.

The Power to Change

On July 24, 2010, I met the group from the discipleship school down at the beach. Sure enough, it was a more intimate and relaxed event—people were playing volleyball and barbecuing. I was introduced to Ricky Page, the pastor who would be baptizing me. He explained what baptism was and how it would go. He said before we can identify with new life in Christ, we have to identify with His death. As you go under the water, you're letting your old life die, but as you're raised up out of the water, you are born again into a new life and a new identity through Christ.

I didn't know how all that would play out, but I was ready. The moment came, and I waded out to where Ricky stood in the water. The baptism itself was over before I knew it. But when I came out of that water, I felt as if something had changed. Something profound had happened.

At that time, I was seeing a chiropractor three days a week to fix a back tweak from a pretty bad accident about a year before. Dr. Klein and I usually engaged in small talk while I was being adjusted, but he was a Scientologist and I had some judgments about that, so I kept our conversations pretty superficial.

The Monday after I got baptized, I went in for my usual appointment. Typically, Dr. Klein asked me how my weekend was, but that Monday he asked, "What happened to you last weekend?"

"What do you mean?" I asked. "I went to the beach with some friends on Saturday. Hung out on Sunday. What about you?"

"Is that it?" he asked.

"Yeah." I didn't see how mentioning the baptism could be relevant or interesting to him.

That Wednesday, I went in and he asked again, "You going to tell me what happened to you last weekend?"

"I already did," I replied, a little confused and annoyed. "I went to the beach and hung out with friends."

"Sure," he said sarcastically.

"What a weirdo", I thought.

That Friday, he asked the same question, with a little more insistence. At this point, I was starting to get curious about what he was digging for, but I still couldn't imagine that the other details about my weekend would be significant to him.

Yet the following Monday he asked again, "Morgan, what's it going to take for you to tell me what happened last weekend?"

"Doc, I already told you three times what I did. I don't know what more I can tell you. I went to the beach with some friends, we had a barbecue and played volleyball, and we went in the water. Sunday we just hung out."

After a moment, he replied, "After I adjust you, can I walk you out? There's something I want to talk to you about."

"Okay, sure . . . I guess," I agreed.

Dr. Klein's office had an open area in the back with three adjusting beds, a short hallway with offices on either side, and a front reception area. After my appointment, we started walking down the hallway. When we reached the first office, Dr. Klein pushed me inside and closed the door behind us. As the two of us stood awkwardly in the tiny examination room, I started to feel anxious. I'd never seen this side of Dr. Klein. What was he going to do or ask?

He looked me straight in the eye with a serious, but sincere expression. "I'm sorry, Morgan, but I need you to tell me what happened to you weekend before last."

"Okay." I started, "But, I told you already. On Saturday I went to the beach with some friends. We played volleyball. We barbecued. We went in the water and I got baptized. Is that what you wanted to know? Why have you been so insistent?"

"Morgan, I've been adjusting you for a year," Dr. Klein explained. "I know your body, I know your patterns, and I thought I knew you. Last Monday when you came in, though, I didn't recognize any of that. It's as if you were a completely different person. Your body didn't even feel the same. To tell you the truth, this past year I've thought you were a bit of an arrogant dick. But strangely, since the other weekend my assistants and I both have been looking forward to you coming in every day. You were a major topic at our staff meeting. It's something I can't explain. In all my years as a chiropractor I've never seen anything like it, and I had to know. I'm not a religious person, Morgan, but whatever you're doing, please keep it up."

I was blown away, and totally overwhelmed with emotion. I couldn't say anything—I just walked out to my car and started to weep. I knew what was happening to me was real, but here was this chiropractor I didn't really know, who I didn't really like, and who I had really judged, seeing something so profound happen in me that he was willing to put himself in an incredibly awkward spot to find out what it was.

✺

I had been working with the global creative director from a Fortune 50 tech giant who was grooming me to take over his position at the company and help him build a creative agency. I had worked my entire career for this kind of high-profile position, with money, recognition, and the kind of big-budget projects that people in my field dream about. At the same time, I saw a video advertising our church's discipleship school, which was a one-year, full-time ministry school focused on global missions. I felt called to go to the school, but battled in my mind as to whether it was a good decision.

I fasted and prayed, and an answer I really didn't want came back.

You can take this job and find success in it, and your life will end and it will have meant nothing. Or you can trust Me and the plans I have for you that are far greater than this job.

I knew it had to be God, because this was certainly not the choice I wanted to make.

I called the creative director and asked him to dinner. He thought it was going to be a dinner of celebration where I would tell him that I wanted to accept the position. Instead, I told him that as honored as I was that he would trust not only his position at this company to me, but also trust me in leading his agency team, I felt like I was being called into ministry, and I couldn't accept his generous offer.

I left that meeting sure I had made the right decision, while also mourning the life I was walking away from. I had had so much hope in all that. It was something familiar, something I knew, something predictable. Now I was launching out into something so foreign. I knew God had me, but I couldn't see even a foot in front of me. However, I had plenty of money in the bank, felt closer to God than I ever had, and felt like I could be of service to others in a more profound way than ever before. I was walking away from the greatest career opportunity I had ever had, but I knew that I was being directed. I could feel it in every fiber of my being.

That honeymoon period of choosing to trust and obey God was pretty sweet . . . until I was blindsided by an attack. The Friday after I turned down the job offer, I got a call from a former business associate. He called me every name in the book as he accused me of lying to him and cheating him. It was a giant misunderstanding, but there was no talking to him in his state. He threatened me physically and promised to destroy my reputation. Instead of waiting until my emotions calmed down, I took the bait and threatened him back. As I yelled at him, terrible thoughts started filling my mind.

I had loaded up my work schedule prior to starting school so I'd have money in the bank to tide me over while I went to school full-time. The weekend after the altercation with my former associate, I decided I was too busy to go to church. I watched the service online, but it wasn't the same. My heart wasn't there. I hadn't missed church since I went back at Easter.

The unforgiveness I was harboring didn't even come to mind as a reason I had made it acceptable to miss church, but the next week I didn't go either. My bitterness towards my former business associate was consuming my thoughts. Even with everything I had learned about owning my own part, forgiveness, and trusting God, in the moment I couldn't shake it. So even though I kept telling myself I was missing church and withdrawing from community to save for discipleship school and get closer to God, in reality I was getting further and further away from Him.

Since Easter, pornography hadn't even appealed to me. I didn't yet see it as something I shouldn't be looking at—I just had no desire for it. But while working these long hours and harboring this resentment, I found myself being drawn back to it as an escape. For the first time in my life, as I watched these videos, I felt like what I was doing was wrong. Literally no one had ever told me that, but I knew. I felt remorseful afterwards, but the next night I found myself back at it again.

The night before I was supposed to start the school, I took it further. It had been years since I had a hookup or one-night stand, but that night I found myself in an online chat room, and the next thing I knew, I was in bed with a complete stranger. In three short weeks, I had gone from a sold-out Christian to doing something I hadn't done for years and promised myself I would never do again.

I was so ashamed. Those familiar accusing voices were back in my head: *You're such a fraud. I knew you couldn't keep up that act. Just face it. You're f**ked up and always will be. You really are broken. Who are you trying to fool? Church school? Come on. If they knew what you'd done, they never would have accepted you. Just wait until they find out who you really are.*

With those thoughts tormenting me, I couldn't fall asleep until after four in the morning. School started at nine. My alarm went off at seven and I hit the snooze button. 7:09. Snooze. 7:18. Snooze. 7:27. Snooze. Snooze. Snooze. Finally, at 7:54, I turned my alarm off. As I lay there, the accusing, self-defeating thoughts returned with a vengeance. Who was I kidding? I can't escape who I am. Maybe for a time, but I always go back to it. What was I thinking? A church school with a bunch of sold-out, missionary-minded, conservative, born-again Christians? I don't belong there. My family are die-hard Democrats. I don't even know a Republican. What was I going to do in a group of people who took the Bible literally?

I went back to bed. My last thought was that maybe I could tell my creative director friend I had had a change of heart and still take that job.

At 8:09 a.m., I found myself standing at the foot of my bed. I didn't remember getting up, but I was filled with the fear of God that if I didn't get to that school, my life was going to end and mean nothing. I showered, dressed, and got out the door in five minutes flat and arrived at the school at 8:55 a.m.

At nine, worship started. There was no screen with lyrics, I didn't know the songs, I was the only person not singing, and I felt judged. I started to think I'd made a mistake. I stood there for three songs, arms crossed, trying to figure out an exit strategy. I'd already paid the $1,500 tuition for that quarter, but I didn't care. I wanted to leave with every fiber of my being. Instead of walking out, however, I prayed.

"God, if You want me here, make a way. Change my heart."

Immediately, the song changed. I started to sing in worship, I raised my hands, and I felt home.

༄

I found out that the first thing we were doing as a class was a week-long hike across the island of Catalina. We spent the first week of school in preparation for the hike, getting to know the people in our groups. That semester there were seventy-two new students at the school—forty-eight in the day program and twenty-four at night. The students were split into smaller groups of twelve called "small families." They were the ones we would camp, hike, and learn with over that week-long adventure.

In my small family, there were two girls with food issues—one had a wheat allergy and one was diabetic. I offered to make raw, vegan, wheat-free food for both of them. Between their food, my food, and all the other stuff I was required to bring, my backpack weighed 136 pounds. Little did I know that we were taking the most difficult route across the island, up and down extraordinarily steep paths, or that the whole trip was designed to break us down so we could be built back up, in love, as we studied the book of First John.

When we arrived on the island, it was around two in the afternoon. We made a short hike to our initial camp spot, set up camp, did some team-building exercises, ate, and began our study. I started to get to know several of the other students, and it quickly became clear to me that though we all had our stories, mine was pretty different from the others. In my small group of twelve, there were three virgins! I never had met anyone who was legitimately saving themselves for marriage before. I thought the only reasons anyone would still be a virgin past their first year at college was because they were ugly, disfigured, or extraordinarily socially awkward. These people were none of those things. They were attractive, engaging, and really wonderful. I started to feel sadness for the way that I had lived.

The second day was our first full day of hiking. We hiked over nine miles and camped at a spot called Little Harbor. That night, we shared our testimonies around the campfire. I was one of the first to share, and I was worried I'd be kicked off the island if everyone knew all that I'd been through, so I shared the easy testimony—that I was a teenage drug addict and alcoholic, and that God had delivered me from that. He had done so much more, but I wasn't sure they'd accept me if I told them about it.

The guy sitting next to me was wearing a house-arrest ankle bracelet. I'd learned that he was a pastor's kid, married to a beautiful woman, father to two handsome sons, and was really clean-cut. I was sure that he had been arrested for inadvertent tax evasion or some white-collar mistake. Then he shared his testimony. It wasn't white-collar crime at all. He had gotten mixed up with an underage girl online and had been arrested as part of an FBI sting targeting child predators. He talked about the miraculous way God had worked out forgiveness with his wife and given him favor with the law enforcement authorities who let him come on this trip. It was an incredible story of redemption, and I regretted not sharing more of my story.

I was starting to connect with the rest of my class, but something still felt like it was missing. There was still hardness in my heart.

On the fourth day, we had a "solo" day with God. The leaders led us out in the middle of the night with just our Bibles and a tarp, bottle of water, headlamp, shovel, and notebook. We spent eighteen hours in solitude. I honestly had no desire to read the Bible, so I slept the first three hours. Once the sun rose around six, I couldn't sleep anymore. I tried to pray, but all my prayers felt insincere, like I was just going through the motions and no one was listening. Once I ran out of things to do to entertain myself, I finally caved and decided to start reading.

I honestly had never read the Bible before. I had read dozens of books about Christ and the Bible, but aside from reading a few pages from First John on this trip, I had never opened the Bible itself and just read. I had no idea where to start. Finally, I decided to begin with the New Testament and opened to Matthew. A few chapters in, I came across these verses:

"You have heard that it was said, 'You shall love your neighbor and hate your enemy.' But I say to you, love your enemies, bless those who curse you, do good to those who hate you, and pray for those who spitefully use you and persecute you, that you may be sons of your Father in heaven.[4]"

I was still holding onto unforgiveness and bitterness towards my former

---

[4] *Matthew 5:43-45*

business associate. I didn't think I could even squeeze out a sincere prayer for him, but I also really felt I needed to. I asked God what to do.

"God, I want to care. Please show me Your heart for him. Show me what to pray."

A thought came, "Start by praying for his soul."

I did. I started praying for his soul, and it opened a floodgate. Half an hour later, I was still praying for him, crying out in a way I had never been able to before. Then I kept praying for everyone in my life, Christian and non-Christian. I prayed for freedom, redemption, love, peace . . . I didn't know where it was coming from but it felt like God was praying through me. Tears of joy ran down my face. I prayed for over four hours straight, and the time flew by. Afterwards, I was so excited to keep reading. I made it all the way through Matthew, and then I just sat in awe of God and thanked Him for letting me get to know Him better that day.

On the way back to camp, the world looked so much more beautiful. I felt so much closer to everyone. I told one of the leaders what had happened. She told me my experience was the whole reason they brought us there, just to learn how to love. I felt so privileged to have understood. 1 John 4:19—"We love because He first loved us"—had begun to come alive for me. There had been a love that seemed so out of reach for me—a connection part of me knew was possible, but could never experience. But now that love made sense and filled me. Coming back from that island, I felt like I was a changed man. However, I still had so much room to grow.

CHAPTER 9:
School for Fools

The discipleship school was radically different from anything I had experienced in my life so far. I didn't know anyone who was politically conservative. I certainly wasn't friends with many people who had been Christians their whole lives and thought the greatest thing you could do with your life was to preach the gospel around the world. I was much more familiar with people in the New Age, Buddhist, and "Coexist" crew, who mostly thought that politically conservative, evangelical Christians were the epitome of what was wrong with the world. I had thought that too. Yet there I was in a giant group of those people, feeling more loved, accepted, and encouraged than I had my entire life.

However, this love, acceptance, and encouragement looked entirely different than what I had previously known. Most of my friends and I had acted as though love meant having a blanket "live and let live" attitude towards everyone. Telling someone they were wrong was inherently small-minded, hateful, and judgmental—this is one of things we judged Christians for doing. But the Christians around me were showing me that if you truly love somebody, you'll actually say something when you see them heading down a path that leads to ruin. If that person doesn't respond to what you say, you don't ostracize them. You pray and fast for them, keep loving them, and trust that God's love will bring that person back to life.

I also saw a completely different model of romantic love and marriage than I'd ever experienced before. I'd always looked at love as a feeling that added to my life, and at romantic relationships, not as a place where I was responsible for growth, but where the other was responsible for bringing value to my life. The moment they stopped bringing value, I was planning my exit strategy. Now I was being taught, and seeing through great examples of healthy marriages at the school, that relationships weren't where I should be looking to add to myself, but where I should be looking to die to myself, because that's where the power was.

I asked George, the pastor over the school, how I would know when I was in love. He said it really simply. "You'll know you're in love when you want what's best for her more than what's in it for you."

Wow, I thought, could it really be that simple? Then I asked, "How will I know when I've met the one I'm supposed to marry?"

He said, "Look—while you're dating, you'll be lucky if you see five percent of someone's baggage. You've got to know that your commitment to them, and your ability to unpack the remaining ninety-five percent of that over a lifetime together, is stronger than whatever might come up."

He also explained that there isn't "one" pre-ordained person for me. I actually have the ability to choose, and there is great practical advice on how to choose wisely.

Many things I experienced in those first few months of school were incredible—insights that radically challenged many of my previously unquestioned beliefs, and genuine friendships and community with a deeper connection than I had ever experienced. Other things, however, were really difficult.

One day, the leaders announced that the whole class was going to do "street evangelism." The only street evangelists I'd ever seen were the kind with giant pictures of aborted fetuses and verses about hellfire and damnation hanging behind them as they screamed about repentance at people walking by. They terrified me and were the most offensive of the overly religious fringe-group Christians. To me, "street evangelism" represented everything I had ever thought was wrong about Christianity and I wanted nothing to do with it. I had already been stretched in my thinking and openness to new practices, but this was a step beyond a step too far. To make matters worse, we were told that our group was going to the Gaslamp District at lunch time. In my eighteen-year career in advertising and design in San Diego, almost all the agencies I had worked for had offices in that area. All those people ate lunch in restaurants on the streets where we were meant to be doing this street evangelism.

When I heard that, I told my leader, "There's no f**king way. This is bulls**t! If this is what this school is about, I don't want to have anything to do with it. Do you realize how many people I know down there? What will they think? I'm fine with them knowing I'm a Christian, but it's not going to be like this!"

In my frustration, I started tearing up. I was so heartbroken that they would force us to do something so awful.

As I started to leave, a girl from my class named Gia ran after me. "Morgan, I've done this before, and I promise, it's not what you think," she assured me. "We don't have to tell people that they're going to hell, or try to make them feel bad about their life choices. We're just taking a survey for the church, asking people if they had an opportunity to ask God one question what it would be. I can partner with you. If you don't want to talk, you don't have to. Just please come. I promise it's not going to be anything like you think, and if you get uncomfortable, we can leave."

I really didn't want to quit the school. I was just scared. Gia had given me the out I needed, so I agreed to go, though I was pretty sure I was going to hate it and want to leave in the first five minutes.

The route we were given was down the busiest streets during the height of the lunch rush. Strangely, it seemed wherever we walked, we saw tons of people walking on the other side of the street, but our side of the street was almost empty.

The Power to Change

We were standing at a corner waiting to cross the street when a Middle Eastern man came up to us and asked the time. Gia engaged him in conversation, explaining that we were from a church and were asking people what they would ask God if they had the opportunity to ask one question. He said he would ask God how to achieve world peace. Gia called me over and then asked him if there was anything we could pray for him for. He explained that he and his wife had just opened a restaurant, and asked us to pray for God's favor over the restaurant, as well as peace for his wife from the stress of opening the new business. After we prayed, he thanked us with tears in his eyes, saying that in his whole time in America, no one had ever offered to pray for him before. As he walked away, he turned back and said, "May God bless you."

That was so much less awkward than I thought it would be, I thought. In fact, it had been wonderful. We had simply had a friendly conversation and prayed with a very nice Muslim man. I felt uplifted, and I knew we had made a positive impact on him too. I looked around and noticed that the three corners across from us were all bustling with people, but while we had been talking and praying with that man, not a single person had walked by us. It seemed like God had literally parted the seas of people for us so I didn't have to feel awkward.

"I see a 99¢ store on the next block," Gia said next. "I feel like God is telling me we need to go there."

"I don't think we're supposed to be shopping," I replied. "I think we're supposed to be talking to people."

"I don't want to shop," she laughed. "I think God's telling me that we need to talk to someone in there."

We walked into the store and started to wander the aisles. It was crowded, and I didn't share Gia's intuition that we were supposed to be there, so I started to feel awkward. But then Gia ran up to me and said, "Come here—there's someone I want you to meet." I followed her up to the cashier. "This is Anthony," she said, introducing us. "This is his store.

He's from Tel Aviv."

I noticed Anthony's watch. It was an Audemars Piguet Royal Oak, almost identical to the one I was wearing. "Nice watch," I said appreciatively, holding up my wrist to display mine.

"No way!" he exclaimed. "You have the same one!"

It was an instant bond. We struck up a conversation and I told him we were from a church, and told him about the survey we were conducting.

"If I could ask God one question, it would be, 'Why are so many religious people hypocrites?'" said Anthony. Then he laughed and said, "I mean, not you guys, obviously. I mean in general."

Gia and I took turns explaining our understanding of the difference between having a religion and having a relationship with God.

"I've never heard anyone talk like you two talk before," Anthony responded. "Where does your chabad (home church) meet? Can I come to a meeting?"

We told him about our school and church and exchanged information. Customers had started to line up to check out, but he turned to them and said, "Give me a second. I'm talking to my friends."

We asked if we could pray for him.

"Yes, please," Anthony nodded. "I would like to find more people like you that I could talk to." After we prayed, he thanked us. "I'll call you. Thank you again!" he shouted to us as we left.

Once again, I thought, *This is so much easier than I expected.*

Next, we walked up 5th Avenue to Broadway, the busiest street in Downtown. As we neared the corner, Gia saw two young Mexican guys covered in gang tattoos standing at the bus stop.

"I think we're supposed to talk to them," she said.

"I don't," I scoffed, shaking my head. "The guys we talked to already were really nice. These guys don't look nice at all. Let's quit while we're ahead."

"Morgan, what's wrong with you?" she said, exasperated. "You stay here, then. I'll go talk to them."

"Fine . . ." I said, unsure about letting her go. "Good luck with that." I stood back watching, and was amazed to see that within thirty seconds, Gia had the two young men smiling and laughing. She called me over, I introduced myself, and we asked them the survey question. It turned out that they had grown up with Catholic grandmothers but had never gotten into church. I shared part of my testimony with them, and they shared parts of their stories with me. Soon they were opening up about some really deep, vulnerable stuff, right there in the middle of the day on a crowed corner on the busiest street in town. Gia asked them if they wanted to pray with us to accept Jesus into their lives. They both said yes.

Was this really happening? I couldn't believe it. As we prayed with these guys, I felt like there was no place in the world that I would rather be. I didn't care who might walk or drive by and see me. This was more important than anything else in the world. As this feeling struck me, I caught myself. Did I really just think that? Have I really become that guy? Wow. I didn't see this coming.

By the end of the prayer, we were all in tears, laughing, crying, and hugging. It was a scene . . . but it was wonderful.

Gia and I said our goodbyes and walked back to meet the rest of the group. Everyone had great stories to share, but none as amazing as ours. God was doing something wonderful in me. Until that point, my faith had been something so private. It wasn't that I was ashamed of it—I hadn't gotten to the point where I was comfortable sharing it, even with my closest friends. Now I felt this fire bubbling up in me and I wanted to share it with everyone—not in a pushy way, but in the natural and easy way I'd experienced in the conversations we'd had that day.

Gia and I continued to partner in our street evangelism outings and became great friends. Soon, God began highlighting people to me when I was out around town. I'd see a person and He'd say, That person is going to know Me today. I'd go and engage them in conversation. I was never pushy about faith, but every time a person was highlighted to me and I talked to them, they led the conversation toward God in some way. If I was out with Gia, I would bring them over to her, and she prayed with them. If I was on my own, I wasn't comfortable asking them if they wanted to pray, but I invited them to church. Every one who came went forward for the altar call. Over the course of the next couple of years, over a hundred people became Christians that way.

During first few months of school, I had some issues with fatigue, interrupted sleep, and short-term memory loss. I looked up my symptoms online and began to worry that my former crazy lifestyle had finally caught up with me. I hadn't been to the doctor in forever and worried that in my promiscuity I had contracted an incurable STD. According to the Internet, the possibilities included HIV, Stage 3 syphilis, and a number of others. I was terrified, but even in my fear, I knew God had a plan.

I started praying and asking for prayer, though I was still too scared to really put the details of my past out there. I also went to the doctor. Because I was a new patient, she ordered a routine physical and some blood work. Looking at the panels she wanted to check for, I asked her to do a full work-up just to be on the safe side. I didn't tell her my fears, just my symptoms.

Waiting for the results was nerve-wracking. I was told they would take a week. I don't know if I ever prayed harder than I did that week, but I did finally find peace through prayer. When I got the call and went in to see her, I knew that whatever I was going to find that morning, God had my back. I sat in the waiting room relieved that I was finally going to have some answers.

They called me back and took my vitals. Then the doctor came in and started to share the results. "Well, obviously, you don't have any of the

STDs," she began with a laugh, as if she had assumed I wouldn't. "Most of this looks pretty good, actually . . . until we get down to your liver, cholesterol, B-12, D-3, and calcium. It looks like you have elevated triglycerides, elevated cholesterol, and the lowest B-12 reading I've ever seen. Are you vegan, by any chance?"

"Yes, a raw-food vegan," I replied, my curiosity piqued. "I have been for ten years."

"Well, a vegan diet is fine for some, but it doesn't look like it's working for you," she stated. "You're not getting any cholesterol from animal products, so if I were to guess, your liver is overworking to produce cholesterol and running inefficiently. You are eating too many carbs that are getting stored as fat, and though you're not outwardly overweight, you have the beginnings of what could become fatty liver disease. You're probably eating too many leafy greens and have more calcium than you need. It's leeching into your blood and preventing the natural absorption of D-3 from the sun. All of these factors are contributing to your blood pressure being slightly elevated as well. You're probably not going to like this, but I'm going to suggest you start eating red meat and getting some serious supplementation from a nutritionist, because the way you're headed, your diet could kill you."

I was stunned. My diet? That was literally the last thing I thought would be the cause of my symptoms. In my mind, I had the healthiest diet on the planet.

The doctor continued, "I'm going to put you on B-12 shots twice a week, suggest you stop eating spinach and kale for now, and start eating fish or red meat at least once a day, with red meat at least three times a week."

Before I left her office, she gave me a B-12 shot and told me to go eat a steak.

I couldn't believe the problem was my diet. All the symptoms had pointed to much worse, and to come out unscathed after the way I'd lived brought me close to tears. It wasn't the best report, but I didn't have any deadly disease. I had been so scared for so long that I had avoided doctors like the plague. I didn't want to know. So much of that fear had kept my life on hold. Now, as my faith started to feel like a foundation I could build my life on, I no longer wanted to run from my past or my fear. I wanted to run straight into them, because I was starting to realize that my God was stronger than any obstacle I could possibly face.

The Power to Change

CHAPTER 10:
You're Not All-In

When I turned down that big job offer to attend discipleship school, I had called my good friend and client, Frank, to tell him what I was doing. He soon came to me with an offer to put me on a monthly four-thousand-dollar retainer if I could guarantee him thirty hours a month for whatever he needed. It was an answer to prayer—I would be able to go to school and not deplete my savings in the process. I also loved working with Frank, and was excited to be able to maintain that relationship. We had known each other for over twenty years, were great friends, and had worked together on several important projects.

But then school started and I never heard from Frank. I left a few messages to check in, but never got a call back. I also reached out to his wife, who had also been a friend since childhood, but she didn't respond either. I had no idea what had happened, and finally concluded that the deal was off. I was disappointed, but was more worried about our friendship than I was about work.

Meanwhile, no other freelance work came in. Clients I'd had for years who always called at least once a month weren't calling at all. It was the driest season for work I had ever had, though it was the richest season spiritually.

I started school with a good amount in savings. I had just been paid on a big job and believed I'd have money coming in. I paid off my $4,500 tuition, paid for mission trips, and was generous with money to friends in need. Six months later, however, I had no work or checks in sight.

On Sunday, April 3, 2011, I looked at my bank account balance and saw that I had $73.06. I drove to an ATM that dispensed tens and pulled out seventy dollars so I could at least get some food. I had enough gas to last me through the middle of the week, but I had no idea how I was going to make it beyond that.

I stopped to get myself a burrito on the way to church. As I sat in the car eating it, I asked God some questions. "Why would You call me to a school and then not provide for me? I've completely derailed my life to follow You—and don't get me wrong, it's amazing—but are You seriously not going to provide for me? Where are You?"

I saw that my burrito had leaked onto my shirt. Great—now I had to go home and change before church. When I got home, I found an envelope taped to my door. Inside were eight hundred dollars in cash, and a note from a guy I had given money to almost a year before to help pay off a debt.

"Sorry it's taken me so long to pay you back," he wrote. "Words can't express how much your generosity affected me—not just in getting out of debt, but in believing what was possible. I'm sorry I missed you today. I hope we get to connect soon. There are so many incredible things happening in my life that I want to share with you. I love you, man. Thanks for everything."

I never expected to get that money back—I had told him it was a gift. Somehow, on the day I needed it the most, it showed up, taped to my door. This would tide me over for a while. I looked up at the sky and said, "Thanks, God."

The Power to Change

When I got to church for the evening service and walked in the lobby, I couldn't help noticing a thirty-foot painting of an overflowing glass of water. On the water glass, the word "BLESSED" was written in big black letters. I guessed it must have something to do with the sermon series they were starting, though they hadn't announced the topic like they usually did.

Wow, how perfect, I thought. I am blessed. Thanks, God.

After talking to some friends in the lobby, I headed into the service. Just as I stepped into the sanctuary, I felt God talk to me. When God speaks to me, it's not a booming voice from above. It's usually thoughts nothing like my thoughts that crowd out all my other thoughts, and suddenly they're all I can think about. They're usually very specific.

"You're not 'all in' with Me, and until you are, I can't use you in the way I want to."

That's all He said. I knew "all in" was referring to my finances, and that He was asking me to give all eight hundred and sixty-three dollars in my wallet. I was not on board.

"Why would You give this to me just to take it away? I argued. Haven't I given enough? I turned down the greatest job offer of my life to spend time with You, serve You, and study the Bible. I haven't worked in six months. If I give this to You, I won't have anything left."

"You're not 'all in' with Me, and until you are, I can't use you in the way I want to."

D*mn it.

I walked into the service. Worship was starting. At my church, the service had the same format every week. We began with three worship songs, followed by announcements, tithes and offerings, a fourth worship song, and the message. Throughout the first worship song, I wasn't happy with what I felt God telling me to do. During the second song, I was warming up. By the end of the third song, I still wasn't happy about it, but I was willing.

The third song started to wind down, and I knew they were getting ready to pass the offering buckets. I thought, Okay, God, I trust You, and reached into my pocket to grab my wallet. But the song didn't stop—the band went right into the fourth song. When that song finished, the pastor came out and went straight into the message. They didn't take the tithes and offerings.

God, are You messing with me? I wondered. Was that a test? Did I pass? What's going on?

The pastor started the message and then stopped. "Oh, I bet you thought we forgot to pass the tithes and offerings. We didn't. And I bet some of you are wondering what this sermon series is about, and why we didn't announce it. They're related. You see, I knew that if I announced a sermon series on tithing, half of you wouldn't have shown up. But for the next three weeks, that's what we're going to talk about. God loves a cheerful giver, and I decided to change up the service and do tithes and offerings at the end. Hopefully God will speak to your heart during this service and by the end you'll want to give cheerfully. If you don't, keep your money. God doesn't want your money. He wants what it's attached to—your heart."

I couldn't believe what I was hearing. The pastor had directly just confirmed what God had said to me. I was awestruck. Over the course of the service, it became clearer and clearer. By the end of the service, I was excited for the offering buckets to come around.

All right God, I'll test You in this. I do what You told me to do. What are You going to do with it?

I threw everything in my wallet into that bucket. Immediately, I regretted my decision. I didn't even keep money for gas or food. I didn't have food in the fridge. Could I run to the end of the aisle, grab a hundred out of the bucket, and tell the usher I had made a mistake? No, that would be too embarrassing. What was I going to do? I had just had this giant spiritual epiphany, acted on it, and right away been filled with fear.

After the service I helped clean up, hung out with friends in the lobby, and left around 10:30 p.m. On the drive home, I started to worry again about money. Then I remembered that about six months earlier, I had bought a car wash at the gas station near my house. I had paid $12.99 at the pump, then discovered the wash was under construction and I couldn't use my wash code. When I went inside for a refund, the clerk had said that only the manager could do returns, and she was only there Monday through Thursday between 9 a.m. and 1 p.m. Those were school hours, so I hadn't had a chance to go back. But now school was on a break, so I could go in the next morning.

As I neared the gas station, however, a thought came. Go in now and return the car wash. She's there. It was almost 11 p.m. on a Sunday night. I thought, No way, but the first thought came again, stronger—Go in!

I sheepishly walked into the gas station and saw a woman at the counter I had never seen before. "Hi," I began. "I bought a car wash about six months ago when you started construction, and I was told that only a manager could do a return for me. I've come in a few times since then, but there hasn't been a manager around. Could you help me?"

She smiled and answered, "I'm actually the manager. Two of my guys called in sick tonight so I had to come in and cover their shift. I'd be happy to return it for you. Sorry for the inconvenience."

She handed me thirteen dollars. I thanked her and left.

I thought, "God, You're good!"

I look at my watch. 11:00 p.m. Where was I going to get food? Normally, the restaurants on my street were all closed by now on a Sunday night. But as I drove down the street, I saw that the doors to the Mexican restaurant, which was the only place I could afford anyway, were wide open. The sign on the door said they were supposed to close at 7 p.m. I walked in and found the chef and the cashier inside. I didn't ask why they were still open—the night had been so weird already that I figured

The Power to Change

I'd just be grateful. I ordered two tacos to go for $3.75 and went home.

As I sat eating my tacos, a sudden and seemingly random wave of inspiration hit me. I remembered this quote by Michael Jackson: "If you enter this world knowing you are loved and you leave this world knowing the same, then everything that happens in between can be dealt with." It struck me how sad it was that he had died broken and lonely, trying to get some sleep, but in the moment of his death, all the negative things people had said about him—all the accusations and negative judgments—were swept away, and all anyone could say was how wonderful he was, how talented he was, what a gift he had, and what a tragedy it was that he was gone.

I realized that memories are made perfect in death, but it only benefits those who are left behind. How much better would it have been if Michael Jackson had known how loved he really was before he died? I started thinking about other icons who had died young, and how so many of them had been judged. I thought about how one-dimensional our culture's views on our cultural icons are. We see them as their public persona, but there is so much more to them than that. There is the way they see themselves and the way they came into this world as children—the way God sees them.

This streak of inspiring thoughts culminated with the idea to create a series of paintings capturing these three perspectives of iconic people—actors, musicians, political and sports figures—who had died. I would call it "Too Late for Goodbyes." I never had a concept for a series before. I had made a few one-off fine-art pieces in the past, but considered myself more of a designer than a fine artist. I was so excited to see how the series was going to turn out that I started sketching immediately. That night I worked out five studies—Marilyn Monroe, Elvis, Sid Vicious, Kurt Cobain, and Frank Sinatra. I also tried to finish Michael Jackson, but it wasn't coming together, so I went to sleep.

The next morning, I woke early and full of energy despite my late night. I walked to my favorite local coffee shop to get a muffin and tea before continuing to work on the paintings. As I walked up, I saw skateboarding legend Tony Alva sitting by himself. I had met him once years before and doubted he'd remember me, but just as I was thinking that, he motioned to me and said, "Your name's Morgan, right? You want to join me?"

Did I want to have breakfast with Tony Alva? Of course I did. Tony was a childhood hero of mine. We sat and talked for two hours about God, recovery, and art. Then he noticed my sketchbook and asked me what I was working on. I told him about my inspiration from the night before and showed him what I'd done so far.

After skimming through my drawings, Tony explained that he owned a gallery in Long Beach and said he'd love to show my work when I finished the series. I was blown away. We exchanged numbers, he left, and I went inside for a refill on my tea.

"Was that Tony Alva?" asked Amanda, the owner of the coffee shop.

"It was," I grinned.

"What were you guys talking about for the past two hours?"

"Life, death, God, art . . . you know, the usual."

"I know you're a designer, right? Do you do art too?" she asked, spotting my sketchbook.

"I do. I just started on a series last night. Want to see?"

"I'd love to."

I started showing her what I had been working on and explained the concept to her. As she flipped through the drawings, she started to cry.

"I'm sorry, but these are beautiful. They're really powerful," she said. "I don't know if you'd even be willing . . . You know we do art shows here once a month. If you were willing, I'd love to give you a show."

"Of course, I would! I've been coming here since I was eight. All my friends come here. It would be an honor."

"I think we are booked for the next eleven or twelve months, but I'll have the girl who books the shows call you and we'll figure something out."

Just as we were finishing our conversation, an old friend of mine, Hilary, walked up to the counter. She asked what we were discussing and I showed her the sketchbook. She barely looked at a few of the drawings before she burst into tears, excused herself, and walked out.

"Wow, that was weird," Amanda commented. "But I told you they were powerful."

"Thanks," I said, amazed by these emotional responses. "And thanks for the encouragement. Have a great day."

"You too. We'll talk soon, I'm sure."

As I walked out, I felt so encouraged. Is this what God meant? Was this how He was going to use me?

My phone rang, and I saw that it was Jeff, an entrepreneur who had wanted to work with me for over two years, but had no money. He checked in every month or so, saying that he was "just about to get funding," but so far nothing had ever come of it. I was sure I was going to hear more of the same this morning.

"Hi Jeff, how's it going?" I asked.

"Great!" he exclaimed. "I got funding! I have a check for you for $2,500 to get us started, and I want to get started right away. Where are you?"

Miraculously, Jeff was right across the street from where I was standing. As he handed me the check, I couldn't help but be astonished by all the things that had lined up over the past eighteen hours.

When I got home, I checked the mail and found a letter from Paul Mitchell. Inside was check for sixteen hundred dollars and a note explaining that when they did their year-end audit, they discovered they still had an outstanding balance on an invoice I had submitted nine months before. I was terrible at bookkeeping and hadn't noticed the oversight. The timing couldn't have been better.

I drove up to the bank to deposit the two checks. While I was in line, Amanda from the coffee shop called.

"Morgan, I'm so glad you picked up. I know it's a stretch, but do you think you could get a show together by Friday? The artist who was supposed to show this month just got here with his work and it's terrible—nothing like what I thought he was going to hang. I want to send him home."

I had five sketches. Getting a full show together in a week was a crazy idea. There was no natural way I could pull it off, but inside I heard a thought. "Say yes. You can do it."

I worked feverishly for the next four days. I slept very little, but was so inspired. I not only got ideas for the pieces I needed to make—I worked out ideas for thirty more in the series.

When I hung the pieces at the coffee shop at five in the afternoon on Friday, the paint on several was still wet. Immediately afterwards, I went home and passed out. At seven the next morning, my phone woke me up.

"Hello?" I answered groggily.

"Hey, buddy! When did you start painting?" It was Frank, the friend who was supposed to keep me on retainer for his business but had cut off all communication with me after I started school.

"Uh . . . I started Sunday night, but actually painting? Wednesday."

Frank laughed. "Hey, I'm sorry I haven't called. I think I was really wrong about you. I'm so sorry. These paintings are amazing. I'm standing in front of this James Dean painting, and I want to buy it for my wife. How much is it?"

"I haven't really priced anything yet."

"I'll give you four grand," he offered. "But you have to take it out of the show and hang it at our house tonight."

"Sold."

The only problem was that the James Dean painting was the centerpiece to the show. How was I going to tell Amanda that I needed to take it down? The only thing to do was replace it with something equally compelling.

I prayed for inspiration, and it came. The one painting I still hadn't figured out was Michael Jackson. Nothing I had put together so far felt right—everything felt like I was trying too hard to make it work. But now, I saw exactly what it should be. I just had to make it.

I worked all morning, and the painting came together effortlessly. I had been nervous about calling Amanda, but now I was excited—the Michael Jackson piece was perfect and tied the entire show together. I went to the café that afternoon, swapped out the paintings, and drove to Frank's to hang the James Dean piece.

While I was at Frank's, I got a call from someone who was interested in the Michael Jackson and Marilyn Monroe pieces. He asked what they were selling for and I told him the James Dean had just sold for four thousand.

"I'll give you seven thousand for the two of them," he offered. "I'd like to give you a check right away to secure the deal, but you can bring them to me after the show closes. Let me know where I can meet you. I can get you a check this afternoon."

I hung up the phone in disbelief. In just five days I had gone from wondering where my next meal was going to come from to making over sixteen thousand dollars! Not only that—a relationship had been restored and a talent I had never tapped into had been unlocked.

As I was finishing hanging the painting at Frank's, my phone rang again. It was another old friend and client, Robert Cromeans, the global artistic director from Paul Mitchell. He had just seen the show and asked if I'd be interested in working on the branding for Mitch, Paul Mitchell's new men's line. They had another artist working on it, but he felt they weren't quite getting it. When he saw my paintings, he thought, *That's it! That's what Mitch is missing.* He asked me if I would be willing to license the images to launch Mitch in Las Vegas at a big show that coming August. In the meantime, he suspected I'd have my hands full dialing in the brand.

I had always looked at tithing as church money-grubbing. I never considered the effect that giving would have on my own spirit or how it would increase my faith. The Bible says that where your money is, there your heart will be also[5]. I had thought that simply meant you invested in what you loved. Then this week had happened. I knew I had heard from God because everything in me naturally cried out against throwing that money in the basket and tried to justify cutting corners. He was revealing my fundamental lack of faith in Him to provide for me financially. I trusted Him to provide emotionally—I had felt it and seen it—but doubted His ability to provide in the physical. Now, what had happened after taking that one step of obedience to go "all in" with my money was radically stretching my belief of what was even possible. Over sixteen thousand dollars had shown up literally out of nowhere, and a friendship and three working relationships had come together. It was like there had been a drought and everything in my life had dried up. Now where there had been a desert, there was a garden overflowing with life.

This experience cast that verse in the book of Malachi in a completely different, and entirely practical, light:

"Bring all the tithes into the storehouse, That there may be food in My house, And test Me now in this," says the Lord of hosts, "If I will not open for you the windows of heaven and pour out for you such blessing that there will not be room enough to receive it. And I will rebuke the devourer for your sakes, so that he will not destroy the fruit of your ground, nor shall the vine fail to bear fruit for you in the field.[6]"

Just a week after "testing [Him] now in this," God had not only poured

---

[4] *See Matthew 6:21*
[4] *Malachi 3:10-11 NKJV*

out plenty of money to take care of me for the moment, but also work opportunities that would go on to bear fruit for years to come (some to this day). On Sunday, I was excited to see what else God was going to do, so I had no problem throwing $1,610 in the offering basket when it went around—almost twice what I had given the previous week.

When my relationship with Frank got restored, he became my best friend and my best client. Over the next six years, we traveled the world together doing millions of dollars in business for some of the world's largest companies. Frank also helped me launch a career as an artist, exhibiting and selling work at Art Basel, and through my first major solo show, getting work into a museum and two important private collections. The relationship with Paul Mitchell rekindled through that art show brought me into a much more significant role in that organization, helping to launch five large brands for them globally as well as a successful salon chain called Walk-In across the United States.

CHAPTER 11:
Love Letters to My Future Wife

During that time of substantial growth with my art and those major business relationships restarting, school was on a one-month break before the start of my final semester. I still didn't quite know how to balance work relationships, personal relationships, and my relationship with God, and in a moment of weakness, I stumbled with pornography.

Everything had been going so well. I didn't know how I could have fallen. I was the guy in my mentorship group who had been victorious in that struggle. How was I going to go to the guys in my group who had looked up to me and tell them what happened? I couldn't let anyone know. I still had about ten days before school started up again. I didn't have to tell anyone. I just had to make sure it didn't happen again. But it did. Again. And again.

I started thinking thoughts I hadn't thought in a long time, ones I thought I had overcome. *You didn't really think this would last, did you? You're such a fraud. You'll never be good. This is just who you are. You're broken. You're weak. Why even go back to school anyway? It's not going to help you. You're never going to be healthy enough to be a husband or a father.*

These thoughts were relentless. I think the worst kind of defeat is the kind that comes after you think you've found victory. Those negative thoughts were so much louder and so much more believable than telling myself, "You're more than a conqueror in Christ. You're the head and not the tail, above and not beneath. You can do all things through Christ who gives you strength.[7]" I had believed that God's grace could cover an infinite amount of sin, but in that moment, I wondered whether God's grace could cover a particular sin an infinite amount of times.

I wanted to believe, but there was so much damning evidence in front of me of a lifetime of failure, and those accusing thoughts were constantly with me. I could barely stand to be around Christians or be at church. All of it felt so dry. But part of me still believed, and truly I couldn't think of another place to go, so I went.

The Sunday before school started again, it took everything in me just to show up at church. Though I usually wanted to hang out in the lobby, that week I found a seat by myself and waited for service to start. I sat there silently praying that God would soften my heart again. As the service started, the worship band started playing a song that spoke directly to me:

We bow our hearts, we bend our knees,
Oh Spirit, come and make us humble.
We turn our eyes from evil things
Oh Lord we cast down our idols

Give us clean hands
Give us pure hearts
Let us not lift our souls to another

And oh God, let us be
A generation that seeks
That seeks your face
Oh God of Jacob.[8]

---

[7] See Romans 8:37, Deuteronomy 28:13, Philippians 4:13
[8] Charlie Hall, "Give Us Clean Hands," © 2000 sixsteps Music, worshiptogether.com songs.

My hands went up in worship, and something did shift. I knew I needed to come clean to somebody. I had made an idol of my own ability, and my pride was keeping me in bondage. There were so many people in leadership at the school I didn't feel I could go to, though. I don't know if it was them, or just the way I saw them, but I didn't feel comfortable confiding what I was going through with most of them. I worried about being judged and given correction from a place of them talking down to me, not walking it out with me. Truthfully, letting people in had always been a big struggle for me. It wasn't so much that I didn't want to—I just didn't know how. I also struggled with picking the right person, one whom I could not only trust with what was going on, but someone who had real answers and wise strategies that would help.

That night there was an altar call at the end of service. I felt like I needed to go forward, but there were a ton of people I knew at service and I worried what they would think. The pastor asked us all to bow our heads and close our eyes. He led us in a prayer and then asked those who had sincerely prayed the prayer to come forward to the altar. I had prayed the prayer, but I didn't have the courage to go forward. Then I looked up and saw one of the school leaders I respected most, Dave, standing at the altar. I knew I needed to talk to him about what was going on with me. I waited around for him after service, and asked him if he'd be willing to get lunch the next day. It was the day before the new semester started and I didn't want begin on the wrong foot. Even though he was extremely busy, Dave said he'd make time for me.

We met up the following day around noon for Middle Eastern food. As we drove over to the restaurant together, I really, really wanted to tell him what was going on, but I couldn't quite get it out, so I asked him questions about the upcoming semester. Though I knew we had limited time, I held back all through lunch. After I cleared the table, Dave started to put on his jacket to leave, and I knew this was it. If I didn't talk to him now, I was really going to regret it.

"Dave . . . there's actually something I need your help with—something I need to get off my chest."

Dave took his jacket back off and sat back down.

"What's up, buddy?"

"I've been struggling. I don't know how it happened, but I started watching porn again. I've been trying to stop for almost two weeks, and I haven't been able to. I really need help. I've never had accountability in this, and I don't know exactly how that would work, but you're the one guy that I trust. I really want to beat this. It's so tough. I've felt so disconnected."

Dave and I talked for another hour. I knew how busy he was and how much he needed to prepare for the next day, yet he was so generous with his time with me, which touched me. That sacrifice made the seriousness of what I was doing even more real for me.

Dave talked to me about "put-offs" and "put-ons"—that it wasn't just about staying away from porn, but finding what was behind it, what kept me going back, and then finding a legitimate solution to that. It was just like alcoholism and every other addictive, compulsive, destructive behavior I've ever used as an illegitimate solution to a legitimate problem. I had already learned that trying to overcome a destructive behavior just by staying away from it because it's bad for me would end in failure—I would either fail to stay away from the bad thing, or pick up another destructive vice in its place. I believe this is because nature abhors a vacuum. If I go to the ocean drop a bucket into it, the water fills it. When lightning strikes, it burns up all the oxygen molecules in the atmosphere where the fork rips through. Thunder is the sound of all the molecules surrounding the space that the fork of lightning burnt up smashing back together, filling the recently emptied space. If I hollow out a log, the space that was once filled with wood is then filled with air. I can't see the air, but I know it's there, because we don't live in a vacuum. A vacuum can't support life.

As Dave and I talked, I realized the exact same thing had been true in my life. Whenever I wasn't being intentional about finding a legitimate solution to the legitimate problem I was solving with the self-destructive addiction—like solving loneliness with porn, lack of connection, anxiety, and emotional pain with drugs and alcohol, lack of purpose with compulsive spending or codependency, etc.—then I went back to the addiction, or found a new addiction to replace it.

Dave encouraged me by explaining that rounding the corner into the third semester of the school was hard for many people, but that he was committed to seeing this through with me and helping me finish strong. He gave me two wise strategies for moving forward.

First, he explained the practical principle Paul teaches in the fourth chapter of Ephesians: "Let him who stole steal no longer, but rather let him labor, working with [his] hands what is good, that he may have something to give him who has need."[9] What a crazy idea—If I have a problem being so selfish and entitled that I take from someone else, something they worked hard for and deserve, the solution is that I should work hard with my hands, take the result of the labor, which I deserve, and give it to someone that is totally undeserving of it. That's imitating Christ in action. Dave encouraged me to apply this principle by finding an activity that would help me to counteract what I was doing when using porn.

Dave suggested that I install accountability software on all the devices where I used the Internet. I had a lot of those. I put the software on my phone, desktop, laptop, and tablet. If I turned it off or went on a questionable site, Dave would get an email and a text.

Just knowing that if I struggled Dave would know helped a lot . . . for the first couple of nights. I knew, though, that if I was going to be successful, it was going to take more than software—it was going to take real heart change. I was going to have to find out what was behind the

---

[9] *Ephesians 4:28 NKJV*

addiction, and find a legitimate solution to that. As I pondered it, I realized that porn, and really every sexual fantasy, was always a focus on the outer, not the inner person. Fantasizing about people sexually always was about using them to gratify myself. Even if my fantasy included giving them pleasure, it was based in what I thought would be pleasurable to them, not really interacting with them. I thought maybe I didn't understand intimacy. Maybe I was actually terrified of real intimacy, and that living through fantasy with porn, or even living out fantasy when I was promiscuous, was a cheap substitute for real intimacy.

While I was looking at all of this, I remembered an article I had read after Michele and I broke up about drug addicts and alcoholics substituting intensity for intimacy. Addicts look for intense relationships that ultimately burn up and then burn out, rather than building deep emotionally intimate relationships that build slowly, but are much stronger than the other. I had bookmarked the article, so I went back and looked at it.

Intimacy has to do with trust, understanding, and feeling understood. People who are emotionally intimate can reveal their vulnerabilities without fear of being rejected, ridiculed or invalidated. Intimacy is based on emotional safety, acceptance, respect, and a mutual give-and-take. Without self-disclosure, there can be no intimacy—but intimacy requires that self-disclosure be met with empathy. Empathy means recognizing how someone else feels, understanding it, caring about how that person feels, and then expressing that care . . .

"Intensity is being completely lost in the emotion of unreasoning desire. It is marked by urgency, sexual desire, anxiety, high risk choices, and the reckless abandonment of what was once valued. All-consuming euphoria similar to recreational drug use (addictive chemical reactions in the brain) . . . loss of ability to make rational evaluations of what is true, valuable and worthy.[10]*"*

I knew a lot about intensity, but very little about intimacy. I believe that I had wanted intimacy, but I had also been really hurt when I let my heart

---

[10] Adelyn Birch, "Intensity or Intimacy? A Relationship Litmus Test" July 15, 2015, Psychopathsand-Love.com, http://psychopathsandlove.com/intensity-vs-intimacy-a-relationship-litmus-test-2/.

be open enough to give and receive it. I starting thinking that pornography had been masking and confusing a deep need for intimacy that was going unfulfilled in my life.

As I studied more about pornography addiction, it started to make sense. I read an article that broke the addiction down into five phases:

1. Early exposure. Studies showed that most men who get addicted to porn were exposed to it early.

2. Addiction. Though porn may not start off as a regular activity, over time it becomes a regular part of life.

3. Escalation. Initially pornography with one person or one couple may be enough, but addiction escalates to more and more graphic porn. Images of scenes that may have once been seen as disgusting now become exciting. At this stage, the addicted person may start seeking out pornography that goes outside their sexual identity.

4. Desensitization. Eventually, numbness sets in and even the most graphic pornography is no longer exciting. Desperation to feel that excitement again sets in.

5. Acting out sexually. Dangerous, high-risk choices are often associated with this phase of addiction.[11]

I had definitely experienced all five of those phases, and had been back at phase two, terrified to go through it all again. I knew that in my past attempts to experience intimacy, I had put dependency on people ahead of my dependency on God. Desperately wanting things to work out in romantic relationships, I had painted red flags green, and in my pain had defaulted into seeking what was easy—intensity—rather than genuine intimacy. I didn't really understand love either. In discipleship school, I was taught the simple truth that love gives and lust takes. When I looked

---

[11] Gene McConnell and Keith Campbell, "The Stages of Pornography Addiction," FocusontheFamily.com, https://www.focusonthefamily.com/marriage/divorce-and-infidelity/pornography-and-virtual-infidelity/stages-of-porn-addiction.

at porn, I was never looking to give. When I fantasized sexually about someone, I was never looking to give, I was always looking to take.

I also looked to the Bible for answers and read in Romans:

For although they knew God, they neither glorified him as God nor gave thanks to him, but their thinking became futile and their foolish hearts were darkened. Although they claimed to be wise, they became fools . . . Therefore God gave them over in the sinful desires of their hearts to sexual impurity for the degrading of their bodies with one another. They exchanged the truth about God for a lie, and worshiped and served created things rather than the Creator . . . Because of this, God gave them over to shameful lusts. Even their women exchanged natural sexual relations for unnatural ones. In the same way the men also abandoned natural relations with women and were inflamed with lust for one another.[12]

Wow. That explained a lot. It blew my mind that words written in the first century could so accurately describe what I had experienced in the twenty-first century. I thought back to the talk that Dave and I had about the book of Ephesians. If the cure for stealing was laboring with your hands and giving to the poor, what was something I could do that was completely counter to the consuming of other people I had been guilty of with my porn addiction? I had heard about people praying for their future spouse, which sounded great, but I really wanted something more tangible. What about writing letters to my future wife? Instead of gratifying my flesh and finding comfort looking at pictures of someone I could see, what if I wrote letters to someone I didn't yet know or see, telling her why in that moment I was waiting for her?

I bought a journal, kept it under the pillow on the other side of my bed, and started writing in it. I found it really awkward at first and had to battle mocking thoughts like, *This is stupid. You don't really mean what you're writing. You're a fraud!* Then I remembered that the name Satan meant "accuser." Though my intellectual mind had fought against the idea of a devil, I was increasingly aware that whenever I was doing something that would lead to growth or breakthrough, that's exactly when those accusing voices would start.

Temptation usually hit me at night when I was alone. Each time, I pulled out my journal and wrote another letter. For years, marriage had seemed like a pipe dream. I had believed those negative, accusing voices. But now as I wrote, I started seeing marriage and family more clearly than ever before. As I started pouring the most guarded parts of me out on paper, I started realizing that I could actually share those things with another person.

For so long, I had treated sex so loosely. I didn't think of myself as worth waiting for. Losing my virginity had been a race to the finish line. As I wrote these letters, all that changed, and those accusing voices that had been so loud began to be silenced by voices of encouragement. I heard, *You're going to be a great husband and an amazing father. You're a great catch. The wait will be worth it. You're also worth waiting for.* What started as a fight against the struggle eventually became something I looked forward to doing. Instead of writing about why I wasn't acting out and what I was believing for, I started writing my future wife letters about things I couldn't wait to share with her. When I realized what I was doing, I got a feeling that my porn addiction was behind me, as in fact it proved to be.

The heart change I experienced in this process brought benefits to all my existing relationships. Instead of impatiently waiting to speak in a conversation, desperately needing to be heard, I became a much better listener. Instead of looking for opportunities to get, I found myself looking for creative ways to give. I started to see and understand the biblical truth, "What the enemy intended for evil, God will use for good,"[13] in a whole new light.

---

[13] See *Genesis 50:20*

The Power to Change

CHAPTER 12:
The Mission Field of My Heart

The last semester of school was the best of all. Though I'm grateful God kept me free from both temptation and distraction in the first two terms, I felt myself maturing in a whole new way in the final term, taking an active role in working out my faith, both in the God-inspired process of writing letters to my future wife and in pursuing a new level of transparency and authentic connection in my relationships in community.

I wasn't the only one who noticed the change either. Leaders at the school, as well as leaders in my recovery organization, started giving me more opportunities to speak. The school asked me to give my testimony on a video that was shared with our 12,000-plus church members, and to write and share devotional messages to the students. Several large groups within the recovery organization also invited me to speak—one asked me to be a keynote speaker at a 4,000-person conference, and another invited me to lead recovery workshops all over southern Australia for a month.

Graduating students of the discipleship school were invited to apply for internship opportunities at the school, which included outreach, facilities, hospitality, missions, and other teams. I was invited to join the academics team to teach a spiritual disciplines class. I could hardly believe that less than a year before, I had barely opened a Bible, and now God had done such a profound transformational work in me that I was being entrusted to shepherd His flock. What an incredible honor. I took that responsibility very seriously, and as I served well, more opportunities opened up.

One of those opportunities was a month-long mission trip to the Philippines. One afternoon I was at the school office preparing for my class, when I overheard the leaders of the trip conversing about who they wanted to speak at various events.

"All of our best speaking opportunities are on the second half of the trip, so let's divide everyone into two groups," one leader suggested. "We'll send the first group out to speak at the smaller opportunities, and the second group to the large assemblies and community outreaches. The first half of the trip, the good speakers will work on construction projects, which will help them build relational equity with the community, so when they speak there'll already be a connection. The first group of speakers can do construction on the second half of the trip. Sound good?"

"Sounds great!" another leader replied. "So, who are our best speakers?"

"Well, we've got Morgan, of course . . ."

What? They mentioned me first? I felt stunned and honored. I began to imagine doing great things for God—preaching and seeing stadiums of people get transformed. I would be stepping into my calling. This was going to be great—I couldn't wait!

༄

We arrived in Manila and drove by bus ten hours to the remote village of Anda in the province of Pangasinan. There, I learned that I had been assigned to work on a construction team led by a man named James, who was married to a leader from the school. James was not a Christian, but he had a heart for humanitarian aid and experience as a general contractor, so he came on these mission trips for the sole purpose of helping people in third world nations build things they couldn't afford to build on their own. I questioned the decision to put a non-Christian in charge of a team, but I wasn't too worried about it. I would do a good job regardless, and couldn't wait for my chance to speak.

Our first construction project was rebuilding the town police station. Because of my experience designing retail stores, homes, and office environments, I was selected to lead design and materials selection. I went through the rooms, noting and measuring all the damaged windows, broken hinges and door-pulls, and all the small details that, in my mind, make or break a project. After deciding on paint and floor coverings, I made a shopping list and went to buy materials. The leaders gave me a budget, but I didn't mind throwing in a bit of my own money if it was going to make a difference. I coordinated with James to get paint to the team first so they could start working while I focused my efforts on the smaller, detail projects.

The leaders of the trip also asked me to document our projects through photography and video. After finishing each phase of the project, I took a break and filmed what the others were doing. A few times, James made snide remarks about me shooting pictures, asking me if I was done playing with my camera yet, as if I was goofing off instead of working. I got the impression he thought it was more important to work than to have the church toot its own horn about the work. I saw documentation as a way to show those who had invested in the missionaries and financially supported the trip that their dollars brought real impact to the region. I was a little offended by his remarks, but I wasn't going to let it get to me.

At night, we studied the book of Philippians. George, the pastor over the school, was teaching. He had become a mentor to me, and was by far my favorite teacher. Learning from him was such a gift. One of the major themes of the book of Philippians is spiritual maturity—the ability to find and draw strength from the joy of the Lord in the midst of trials. Reflecting on how far I had come in this area was a source of encouragement for me. I knew God had big plans for my life on this trip, and I was ready!

Our first outreach team was booked for several assemblies that were expected to be small, but turned out to be much bigger. Five hundred people showed up to an assembly where they had planned on fifty. Almost none of the attendees spoke any English, and the team didn't have a translator. Miraculously, however, the attendees understood in their own language, and they all responded to the altar call given in English. I thought, *If that is happening with a team of inexperienced speakers, how much more will God do with my team?*

The anticipation of what was to come kept me motivated on my project at the police station, which was going well. The trip leaders commended me on my work, and I was proud of how the station was beginning to look.

By the last day of the project, I had repaired or replaced all the broken windows and doors, repaired cabinets, put down floor covering and finished my detail projects. The rest of the team, however, hadn't finished painting.

How come I finished all of these things by myself and the team of seven who were painting haven't finished yet? I thought. *They need to hurry up. If I was the one painting, I bet I could have gotten the job done much faster.*

I headed over to the site where they were working to offer my help.

"Oh, look who decided to join us," James commented as I approached. "Did you have fun with your little projects and your taking pictures?"

My little projects? I thought indignantly. *The details make the difference, James. What's taking you guys so long?* I kept my mouth shut, though, and just smiled at him. Besides, this project would be over tomorrow, and I'd be able to start doing what I'd really come to do—speaking!

I started painting, but it was a lot harder than I thought it would be. With over ninety percent humidity, the masking tape wasn't sticking very well. I also overloaded my brush and dripped a few times. When James saw my work, he ridiculed me and told me to go dig a trench on another project.

I was officially furious. As the driver drove me to the other project, I thought of all the ways I was going to tell off the leadership about James. How dare they bring a non-Christian, who clearly didn't have God's heart, to lead a team! I rehearsed what I was going to say, and the more I repeated it in my head, the more justified I felt in my animosity towards James.

We arrived at the group of houses where the other project was, and I immediately went looking for Dave, who was co-leading the trip. As I walked up to him with anger in my eyes, he opened his arms and said, "Come here, buddy." He gave me a big bear hug and I broke down sobbing. I tried to explain what was going on, but it was no use. I was overcome with emotion and not making any sense. I offered to work, but Dave told me to go down to the beach to spend some time with God.

I walked down to the beach, confessed to God the judgment I had towards James and the ugliness it had created in my heart, and prayed for forgiveness. After that, I felt a strong need to talk to a friend who was not on the trip. Before I had left the U.S., I had called my cellphone carrier to check the cost to call home. They had said it depended on the area, but most of the islands in the Philippines had a rate of ninety-nine cents a minute. I decided to call my friend Samuel and try to keep it short. We talked and laughed for almost two hours. I knew it was going to be an expensive call, but it was so good to let a friend pray for me and remind me that in all things, God had my back. When I hung up the call, I got a text message telling me that 126-minute call cost $3.99 a minute, for a total of $462.84!

That night at dinner, the leaders announced that our big speaking opportunity was canceled. Instead, we were going to help rebuild a large high school that had been destroyed by a typhoon. I was disappointed, but my consolations were that James was still working on the police station, and that I would be able to have some one-on-one interaction with some teenagers from the local villages who were going to help with the high school project.

The next day, however, I found out that James had been asked to lead the high school project, and I was going to be shooting photography and video. Even though I dreaded James's condescending remarks, I still looked forward to working with and interacting with the locals.

When we got to the high school, I was given a long list of shots that they wanted documented. It took me about three hours to get through them. I was so excited to get to work and get to know the kids who had come to help.

Afterwards, I went to James and asked for an assignment. He looked at me smugly and said, "Oh, you're done playing with your camera? Well, a bunch of locals showed up and there aren't any more brushes or tools. Why don't you run on back to the other project and work on that ditch I told you to dig yesterday."

I wanted to punch him in the throat and scream *"F**k you!"* But I didn't. I didn't want to make a scene. "They'll know we're Christians by the love we show one another"[14] right? Most of all, though, I didn't want to disqualify myself from all the speaking opportunities that lay ahead.

On the ride back home, I almost hyperventilated, swinging between wanting to scream, wanting to cry, and wanting to beat James' head in. I hadn't said anything yesterday, but today I was going to tell leadership that James had to go.

Once again, Dave saw me coming and opened his arms.

"Don't try to hug me!" I half-yelled. "Why is he here? Why is James here? He doesn't know God. He doesn't have God's heart. Why would you put him over a team? He's abusive. He doesn't have eyes to see or ears to hear. If he just had the f**king Holy Spirit living in him, at least he'd feel conviction, but he doesn't even have that!"

---

[14] *See John 13:35*

Wait a sec. I had just said "f**king Holy Spirit" to a pastor. Was I going straight to hell?

Dave just looked at me, smiled, opened his arms, and motioned to me to come give him a hug. I really needed a hug, but I really, really, really didn't want to give him one, because to me it felt like conceding defeat. I was so angry. I just stood there and started sobbing. Dave walked over and hugged me for what felt like an eternity. What was wrong with me? I was a mess. Dave sent me back down to the beach.

I took a Bible with me. Maybe it had the answer. I had been studying in our night sessions and preparing to speak, but I hadn't really been spending any quiet time with God in His Word. I knew that was lacking. I searched the glossary for repentance, and it pointed me to this verse: "Godly sorrow brings repentance that leads to salvation and leaves no regret, but worldly sorrow brings death."[15]

I didn't get it. My heart had been broken yesterday. I thought it was godly sorrow, and that I had repented. But now I was full of regret wondering what was wrong with me.

That night at dinner, I sat and talked with a man named Joseph, a mature Christian who had set up this opportunity for us to be in the Philippines. I shared what had happened over the previous couple of days, not blaming James, but really seeing how my pride had blinded me and caused my offense. Then I brought up the confusing verse with him, explaining that I had repented, and then what had happened that day.

"If you had really repented, would you have done it again?" he asked.

I thought that sounded religious and judgmental, but I knew Joseph, so I tried to think about various things one could repent of and responded, "I don't know . . . I guess it would depend."

"It shouldn't."

---

[15] *2 Corinthians 7:10 NIV*

The Power to Change

I was stunned. "No exceptions?"

He said, "Maybe you don't understand repentance."

"Maybe I don't. What does that verse mean? I've always thought that when I do something wrong, the Holy Spirit convicts me, I confess to God, and pray for forgiveness."

"There's a lot more to it. That's the beginning, but that's not the end of it. Morgan, repentance is a lot like sanctification—it sometimes takes a while, and it has a few parts. Confession, which is mind change, leads to that godly sorrow—we call that contrition or broken-heartedness—which is heart-change, which leads to life change. Did anything change in your life after you felt bad and asked God to forgive you? Did you change your actions towards James? I find that sometimes I have to confess over and over again until I really hear that confession in my heart, and then my heart cries out to God, 'Change me!' That's when I really see my life change, and sometimes it takes time to get there."

I thanked Joseph for the talk and walked down to the beach. It was about ten at night, but the moon was almost full, and the white sand glowed in the moonlight. I sat in that light and asked God to show me how He saw James.

A thought came. *What if James was the one God would leave the ninety-nine to go after? What if this whole trip wasn't about the people on the island, but getting the people from San Diego around James outside the hustle and bustle of life, where he could experience the love of God by the way we treated each other and the way we treated him? And what if God needed me to see the one before He set me in front of thousands?*

Had I really been so concerned about God using my speaking gift that I failed to see the one who didn't know Him standing right in front of me? That thought broke my heart. I wept for my shortsightedness. I prayed that God would give me eyes to see what He showed me that night, to break my heart for James even when he was not treating me well, to not allow offence to bubble up in me, but instead when I got hurt to see it as an opportunity to heal whatever is hurting in the one who just hurt me.

My goal for the rest of the trip was to get to know James. I looked for areas where we had commonality. Instead of coming in with assumptions and a desire to be heard, I came in with questions and a desire to know him. I started to discover that James had a great sense of humor and a big heart for people.

As it turned out, every single one of the "big opportunities" where my team was supposed to speak got canceled. Thankfully, our last event, a Christmas festival and dinner for 5,000 people, which was a combined effort of both teams, was an incredible success.

Instead of being asked to speak though, I was asked to shoot photos and video at the event, which gave me an opportunity to engage with the crowd. One of the people I met was a high school student named Niko. Niko had the most serious expression of any local I had met on the trip. Nearly all the Filipinos smiled as they talked to us, but Niko was completely deadpan. He wanted to know where we were from and why we were there. I asked him questions about his life and what he thought of the event. He told me that he had lived in Anda his whole life and had been raised in the church, but didn't believe. There were things that didn't make sense to him, and he had questions that seemingly no one could answer. I knew what that was like. He politely thanked me for the food, but told me he wasn't planning on staying for the music or the speaker. I told him I understood and asked if I could pray for him. He said no, laughing as though I had made a joke.

Later in the evening, a choir sang Christmas songs and Joseph preached a message. I was positioned on the corner of the stage shooting video and photos of the performers, speakers, and audience. Towards the end of Joseph's sermon, I saw Niko sit down with a group of his friends in the front row. When Joseph prayed and gave the altar call, I saw tears well up in Niko's eyes and stream down his face. Joseph asked if there was anyone who wanted a relationship with Jesus. Hands went up everywhere, but Niko didn't raise his hand. "I feel like there's one more person," Joseph said, and another few hands shot up. After a moment, Joseph continued, "I feel like there's one more person who has a battle going on in their mind. They've been hurt or disappointed . . . and they're really smart. They don't see how any of this could be real."

I looked again at Niko. His face was in his hands, and I could tell he was really crying. Under my breath, I prayed that he'd find comfort in whatever was going on. Seconds later, I saw him look up and raise his hand. He was smiling from ear to ear.

If this trip has only been for him, I thought, *it has been worth it.*

Joseph asked everyone who had raised their hand to come forward to the stage so he could pray with them. Hundreds of people swarmed the stage and I lost sight of Niko in the crowd. I wanted to talk to him and learn what had happened. I had seen a change come over him as he sat there, his face transforming first from his original deadpan demeanor to a pained, sorrowful expression, and then to beaming with joy. I felt like I had find him.

After the event, I looked everywhere for Niko and asked the kids he had been sitting with if they knew where he was, but they didn't. The next day was our last day on the island. It was also our last outreach assembly. The assembly was at a school deep in the jungle, about a forty-five-minute drive from where we were staying. The school was small, and the room for the assembly wasn't large enough to hold everybody. I wasn't one of the speakers selected, so I volunteered to sit outside to allow the last two local children to fit in the assembly.

As I was walking around the school grounds outside, Niko rode up on his bike, jumped off, and came running over to me. I was overjoyed to see him. He had ridden out to where we were staying because he wanted to tell us what had happened to him the night before, and when he found out that we were speaking at this school, he rode his bike all the way there to find us. It took us forty-five minutes by car, and I couldn't imagine how long it had taken him by bike. He looked like a totally different person than the one I had talked to the day before. He was so full of joy. All the seriousness and cynicism he'd had in our previous conversation was gone.

I asked him what had happened during the altar call. He explained that he had been outside because he didn't want to hear the preaching, but came in to find his friends to see if they wanted to leave. They told him it was almost over and encouraged him to stay. As he listened to the end of the message, he became overwhelmed with emotion. Suddenly, things that had seemed ridiculous made sense to him. He said he had always thought Christians were foolish, but in that moment, he realized that he had been the fool. When the pastor had prayed, he felt like the prayer was just for him, but he worried that someone he had mocked for their faith would see him and mock him. When the pastor said there was one more, and then described him, he knew it was God and he couldn't help but raise his hand. He left right afterwards because he had an overwhelming desire to read the Bible. He said he had read the Gospel of John the previous night.

"Morgan," he said, "I read 'And you will know the truth and the truth will set you free.'[16] Morgan, the Truth isn't an idea or a concept. He's a person, and His name is Jesus."

As he said this, tears started running down his face. I was so moved that I started tearing up too. How amazing was it that God could change a heart so profoundly in an instant and give someone who had judged Christians all his life such a deep and mature revelation?

Just before I left on this trip, I felt God say to me in prayer, *"When I highlight someone to you and tell you that they're going to come to know Me, you always bring them to church or to Gia. I want you to bring them to Me.*

---

[16] *John 8:32 NIV*

I hope by now you trust Me enough to do that."

I thought during the trip I was going to be able to lead hundreds of people to Christ, speak before thousands, and experience God in a whole new way. Well, I had experienced God in a whole new way, but it was nothing like I expected. I realized if seeing Niko change was the only reason we had come to the Philippines, it was worth it. I thought about the revelation I had on the beach. What if God needed me to see the one before He set me in front of thousands, because each one of the thousands was equally precious to God? If people's souls ever became just a number to me, I knew I would have no business talking to anyone about God.

The next morning, Niko came to see us off. Though the trip had been nothing like I had expected, I knew I had grown a lot. There had been some necessary pruning, some necessary instruction, and some experiences and people I would never forget.

CHAPTER 13:
An Unwanted Gift

The day I got back from the Philippines, my friend Tommy called and asked if I was willing to teach at a recovery Bible study. I had spoken a lot in recovery settings, but never in a Christian recovery group. I was honored and excited. They were studying the fourteenth chapter of Mark—the part where Peter walks on water. I was grateful for the opportunity, and spent the week preparing. After I taught, everyone came up and told me what a great message I had given. Tommy asked me if I could come back the following week and teach again.

As I was leaving, a young man came up to me, thanked me for speaking, and asked if I'd be willing to mentor him. I told him I may be willing, but I'd like to get to know him before I was willing to commit. I asked him to meet me there the following week when I'd taught again, and to bring his Bible and a notebook.

The next week, he was waiting for me when I pulled up, Bible and notebook in hand. We sat down and I started to talk to him about faith and recovery. It quickly became very clear that he had no idea about either. I felt God say, *"He doesn't know Me. Ask him if he wants to pray."*

What? Right here? I was so nervous. I had never led anyone in that prayer before. I beat around the bush about it for a good ten minutes, then asked him, "Have you ever prayed to receive Christ?"

"No," he said. "But will you pray with me?"

"I'd be honored," I replied.

We sat in my car and I led the prayer. As we finished, we both had tears on our cheeks and I thanked him for allowing me to share that moment with him. We walked into the building where I was going to teach and I ran to the restroom to pray and thank God for what had just happened. As I taught that night, there were several moments where I was overcome with joy, and had to pause so I didn't burst into tears. The feeling in the room was so intimate, and I felt so grateful that God allowed me to be used that way.

Afterwards, a man came up to tell me how impacted he was by my message the previous week. As he was talking, I felt God say, "*This conversation is not as important as the one you are supposed to be having with the young man standing about ten feet behind you. He's been hovering but doesn't want to interrupt. I want you to lead him to Me.*"

I turned around and saw a young man. I excused myself from the conversation I was in and went to introduce myself to him.

"Hi, I'm Morgan."

"I'm Mike. Great job tonight. I got a lot out of what you had to say."

We talked for over an hour, and I felt prompted to ask him if he wanted to pray to receive Christ. To my surprise, he said yes.

I couldn't believe it. *Never before, and then two in one night? What were the odds?*

We prayed and then said our goodbyes. As I walked back to my car, I noticed Caleb and Jeff, two guys from my school, standing in the parking lot looking excited.

"What are you doing here?" I asked, surprised but happy to see them.

"We were just picking up a suitcase for Caleb at an apartment over here, but we saw you praying with that guy, so we thought we'd wait for you. Great job!"

I told them the story of what had happened. I was so grateful for what God had allowed me to do, and celebrating it with two friends magnified my joy even further.

As I drove home, I reflected on how much my life had changed in such a little time. How had I gone from relentlessly making fun of and judging Christians to teaching the Bible and leading lives to Christ? Never in a million years did I think I would become "that guy." It was wonderful.

When I got home, I prayed, thanking God for what He was doing in and through my life. Mid-prayer, something in me took over and I started praying in a language I had never heard before. I had heard people pray in tongues before and it freaked me out. I didn't get it—to me it was the most offensive of the gifts in the Bible. I understood the story of Pentecost, when Peter preached in Aramaic and his audience, who were from a wide geographical area, all miraculously heard him in their own language. In that instance, God had done something miraculous so that these people would understand. But people I had heard "speaking in tongues" sounded like nonsense babble to me, and I just thought they were being weird to make themselves seem spiritual. That night when I prayed, though, I didn't feel like it was something I could even control. I listened to the words coming out of my own mouth, and it sounded like a language—not one I had ever heard, but a language. It went on for forty-five minutes. I didn't know what to do. I had to be at the school at eight in the morning, and needed to brush my teeth and get to bed. But I didn't want to just shove a toothbrush in my mouth. I remembered a Bible verse that said don't quench the Holy Spirit. I didn't know exactly what that meant, but I didn't want to take chances. Eventually the prayer ended, and I brushed my teeth and went to bed.

In the morning, I bounced out of bed around 5:30. It was the first time in forever I had woken up on my own that early. I made myself breakfast and spent some time in prayer. I had barely started praying when the tongues started again. What was going on? I had never experienced anything like it. This time it only lasted fifteen minutes.

I realized that once again, God was stretching my faith and challenging my rational mind. I was grateful for the experience, though, and especially grateful for the experience of being able to join two young men the night before as they made a decision that would impact eternity.

I could hardly wait to get to the school that morning. My friend Caleb was leading a worship service before class. I felt like I had a whole new reason to worship, and a whole new perspective on it as well. I looked around the room at all the students, interns, and staff—there were around two hundred of us worshiping together. One of the songs, "Exalt the Lord," had this incredible harmony. I closed my eyes, overwhelmed by its beauty, and imagined that this might be a taste of what heaven was like—forever in joy, in community, in harmony.

I was teaching my spiritual disciplines class that day. It was incredible to me that hardly a year after opening a Bible, I was entrusted with teaching this foundational class to our students. One of the disciplines I taught on was prayer, and I looked forward to describing the experience I'd that morning and the night before. The textbooks for that class were *Celebration of Discipline* by Richard Foster, and *The Spirit of the Disciplines* by Dallas Willard. As I studied and prepared for lessons, I developed a much better practice of engaging God in ways I had never imagined.

I was sitting in the academics office at the school preparing my notes to teach when my advisor came in. He told me that we had been invited to attend a conference being put on by Renovaré, a group Richard Foster and Dallas Willard had started, at a college campus in San Diego the following week. Richard Foster would be teaching along with a long list of best-selling Christian authors and pillars of the faith. It sounded amazing.

In exchange for admission to the conference, we were asked to volunteer for at least one session over the four days. I had a flexible work schedule and was able to volunteer for all the sessions. The talks were powerful and thought-provoking, but the most inspiring thing to me was seeing every one of the speakers sitting in the front row of every session, no matter who was speaking, with pens and notebooks, expectant to hear from God through their colleagues. There were members of the old guard, like Richard Foster, Chris Hall, the editor of Christianity Today, and Julia Roller, the only author who's ever been approved by the estate of C.S. Lewis to use his *Chronicles of Narnia* in a devotional book, and the new guard like Nate Foster, Richard Foster's son. Every speaker went to every session. No one spoke and then left to play golf or enjoy the beaches of San Diego.

I had never seen any thing like it. At the church I attended, if the senior pastor wasn't preaching, he wasn't in the building. He certainly wasn't in the front row of the service taking notes. The same was true at the school where I taught—none of the pastors had ever attended my class. In fact, the only class the other teachers really ever attended was George's—he was the pastor over the school, and in the opinion of most, the most gifted teacher at the school. I realized that this culture was consistent throughout the church. If the senior pastor was preaching, the parking lot was over-full. If people found out he wasn't preaching, it was over half-empty.

Richard Foster could have easily taught every session at the conference, but it seemed like he was there as much to get filled up as to pour out, and that he was more interested in raising up the next generation of leaders than being raised up and praised for his insights.

On the last day of the conference, Richard approached me during the morning session. "I've seen you faithfully serving here all week," he smiled. "If you're available, I'd love to sit with you at lunch today."

An invitation to lunch from Richard Foster? Of course! I was honored to go.

After we sat down, Richard asked, "What is the biggest new insight you have had this week?"

"Honestly... it was all of you," I declared. "Don't get me wrong—the teaching was amazing. I loved your talks, Chris's talk on working out your faith, and Nate's talk on how God speaks through His written Word in Scripture and in His manifested Word in creation. That was probably my favorite talk. You must be really proud of him."

"Oh, I am," he nodded happily.

"The biggest takeaway for me, though," I continued, "was watching you, Chris, Julia, and the rest of the speakers sitting, writing, and engaging in every single talk no matter who was speaking. It wasn't just honoring—for me it was faith-building. It looked like you all expected God to speak to you through the other speakers. It made me want to listen better and take better notes for fear of missing some gold."

"That's exactly the reason we started Renovaré," Richard replied, his smile widening. "There's been a conversation going on in the Trinity since eternity past, and in community we enter into it. We don't want speakers who come, speak, and leave. If you don't want to be here for all of it, we don't want you here for any of it."

"Man," I said, "If I could find a church that operated like that, I don't think I'd ever leave."

About a week after the conference, the school semester ended and I threw myself into work and art. An art representative had been getting me opportunities, and had found a gallery that was interested in exhibiting my art at Art Basel, one of the world's leading art shows, in Miami. I prepared two large mixed-media works in resin and several smaller pieces for the show. It was a big opportunity. The gallery gave me top billing, and one of my paintings was the centerpiece of their booth.

On the last day of the show, noted collector and New York socialite Jill Sackler, the widow of Arthur Sackler, bought one of my pieces for her collection. It was the largest piece to sell for the gallery that had brought me there and it was a big deal for my career. Also at the show, a woman who owned a gallery in San Diego saw my work and offered me my first major solo show.

I spent the entirety of the next three months preparing for the opening of the show. I took a break from teaching that semester at the school so I could give it my full attention. I soon discovered that I had bitten off a little more than I could chew. Despite working sixteen-hour days and pushing myself as hard as I could to finish, the show opened with much of the work in an unfinished state. I had believed for major success through that show, but also saw where I had really needed help with organization, which I should have asked for, but didn't. It was an incredibly hard lesson.

At the opening, Hugh Davies, director of the Museum of Contemporary Art San Diego, offered to buy one of the pieces for the Museum's permanent collection, and another collector bought a large piece. It was less than I'd hoped for, but it was also encouraging to watch my career grow despite my disappointment.

A few weeks after the opening, I went up to Seattle for a week-long personal development retreat. My health had really suffered from the long days and no rest, and a retreat felt like the perfect solution to that. As it turned out, however, the retreat was more challenging than relaxing. Much of the work we did was around identity, and it involved looking at wounds we had experienced in our lives—some as far back as childhood—and the behavior patterns we had developed from those wounds.

One of the retreat facilitators presented the idea that it's often from our greatest wound that our greatest strength is born. I looked back on the experience I had with my father and the Pianosaurus. When he gave my most prized possession to a little girl, the daughter of a man he barely knew, subconsciously I developed a belief that I didn't have value. My dad didn't value me enough to care about what was important to me. Some little girl he didn't know meant more to him than his own son.

Intellectually, I could find several ways to justify his actions. He was a drunk and it was probably a careless mistake. Perhaps I had gotten caught in the crossfire between him and my mom during their divorce. Or, at best, maybe he really didn't think the piano was that important to me and truly intended on getting me a grand piano. None of these rational explanations fixed the damage to my heart, however.

Doubting that I had value drove me to want to bring value to every relationship I had. At work, I had pursued a career in bringing value to businesses. In the recovery community I had been a part of for over two decades, I had sought to bring value to the men I mentored and help them find their own value. At my best, it was a superpower. But at my worst, I believed that if I wasn't needed I wouldn't be wanted, and living out of that belief had left a trail of broken relationships in my life.

Before I found a relationship with God, I had a long string of relationships with friends, girlfriends, and men I mentored where I subconsciously allowed them to develop a faulty dependency on me. I was completely blind to what I was doing and how destructive this codependent structure was. I had healthy friends who confronted me about that behavior, but I could not see another way to operate. It was so ingrained in me.

Over the course of that week, there were several moments of frustration when I wanted to leave. There were also tears mourning the pain of my past, and joy knowing that in God my identity was secure and I was eternally loved, regardless of my past. God loved me just because He created me to be loved.

CHAPTER 14:
Faithful to Heal

While at the retreat, I started developing sciatic pain in my right leg. I imagined it was because I had run myself down so much while working long hours on my art, and that with some good rest it would go away. It didn't. It got worse . . . much worse. With medication the pain was manageable, but if I forgot to take my pill, I couldn't walk or sit down. The pain was unbearable.

Over the next year, I went to every type of specialist I could find, from sports medicine doctors to acupuncturists, physical therapists, chiropractors, massage therapists, and orthopedic surgeons. I had two MRIs and a half dozen X-rays. No one could find the source of the pain, nor could they treat it. Many of the treatments I had weren't covered by insurance, and cost tens of thousands of dollars.

I also sought out prayer from well-known Christian healers. A friend went to a charismatic church with a popular healing ministry. The church was about thirty minutes from where I lived in San Diego. I went up on a Sunday night to their evening healing service. When the pastor called those in need of physical healing up to the altar, about ten of us went forward, and I was the first to receive prayer.

I hadn't taken my medication that day because I wanted to know if the healing worked. I was desperate—I didn't want to think it worked and then go home to find I was still in pain. As I stood there and the pastor prayed for me, my pain was at a ten out of ten. He prayed and asked me if I felt anything. I didn't. He prayed again and asked. Still nothing. He prayed and asked nine times in total, and nothing happened. The pastor said he had to pray for the others, but he would come back to me—he wasn't me leaving without breakthrough.

As I waited, I felt God say, *"Get down on your face and pray."*

I had never prayed on my face in my life, especially in front of a large church, but I was desperate for breakthrough. It was excruciatingly painful getting down on my knees and then my face to pray. It was also awkward and embarrassing. Desperation is a funny thing, though. At that point I was willing to do anything to get healed.

While I was praying, I heard God again. *"I am faithful to heal you, but you have to let go."*

These words were not encouraging or helpful. *"Let go? Let go of what? Don't You think I want to let go? I certainly haven't held on to money. I let go of that. I want to let go of this pain. I'm not getting anything from it. It's hurting me. I'm here on my face in front of a church in excruciating pain. What the f**k else do You want from me?"*

The pastor came back and prayed for me for a good twenty minutes. Still nothing. Finally, he said, "I'll pray and fast for you this week. Come back next week—we're going to get this thing."

I was so touched, both by his offer to pray and fast, and by his faith that we were going to get this. The next Sunday, there was massive freeway construction on the way to the church, so I was about fifteen minutes late. When I walked in, the church was in the middle of worship, but when the pastor saw me, he stopped the music and addressed me.

"You're the guy with the leg pain, right?" The entire congregation turned around to see who he was talking to.

"Yes," I answered.

"I prayed and fasted for you this week. God told me that He's faithful to heal you, but you have to let go."

"He told me the exact same thing," I said, shocked. "Did He tell you what I needed to let go of? Because I have no clue. I certainly don't want this pain."

"No, just that you had to let go."

I was so frustrated. I left the church after service and went home in pain.

I continued to take medications to manage the pain and did my best to learn to live with it. I believed God could heal me, but I figured I hadn't found the right healer yet. Maybe He would lead me to another person who could help me figure out how to "let go."

⁓

Thursday, December 26, 2013, I was laying in bed at home elevating my leg on these Egoscue pillows that were supposed to help with pain (but honestly weren't doing much), when my phone rang. The call was from Gia, my friend from discipleship school. She said she had a friend named Jenny she wanted to introduce me to. I had never been on a blind date in my life, and had refused every other friend who had ever tried to set me up with one of their friends. But when Gia asked, I had total peace about it.

"Okay, so I'm going to give you her number, but you need to call her. Don't you text her!" Gia admonished.

"Of course, I'll call her," I retorted. "What do you think I'm going to do—text her and say, 'Gia says you're hot. Got any pics?' I'm a thirty-eight-year-old man, Gia. I'm not sixteen."

"You'd be surprised," she laughed.

I called Jenny, but it went to voicemail, so I left a message. She called me back the next afternoon. Our conversation was effortless. I felt like I was talking to someone I had known my whole life. We talked for hours about everything. I don't think I had ever had a conversation flow so easily, especially with a girl I had never met. I asked her if she'd go on a date the next day, and she said yes.

When we met for lunch, we both felt an instant connection. Conversation was deep and not at all awkward. The time flew by. We talked about our lives, histories, dreams, and hearts. When Jenny told me about her community at church, I was intrigued. We arranged to go together the next morning. I figured I could go to her church in the morning, because I usually went to the evening service at mine. We talked, walked, and laughed all day and into the night, finally saying our goodbyes at 10 p.m.

The next morning, I woke up early with the excitement of a six-year-old on Christmas morning. I was supposed to pick up Jenny at 10:30. How was I going to get through the next four hours? At last, the appointed time came. I met her at her house and we drove together to church.

The church was called C3, a plant launched in 2005 by Pastors Jurgen and Leanne Matthesius from a church originally started in Australia. Walking through the lobby, I met at least a dozen people. They all seemed genuinely interested in knowing me—they weren't saying hi just because it was expected of them. Jenny also introduced me to several of her friends. I knew if the service was as good the experience I had just had in the lobby, it was going to be a great morning.

Pastor Jurgen preached a message called "Awaken a Bigger God." He was insightful, relatable, funny, and profound. What I had never seen before in a church, though, was a crowd cheering the pastor on as he spoke and engaging fully with the message. Nearly everyone was taking notes, and when he said something really good or deep, shouts of "So good!" or "Come on!" went up all over the room. I imagined this was probably as close to a Southern Baptist church as I had been so far. Although it was different than what I was used to, it was also fun.

After the service, Jenny and some of her friends invited me to join them for lunch. I found myself at a big table of about twelve people. Everyone was asking lots of questions, but not in a prying way—it felt so inclusive. They were planning a Great-Gatsby-themed murder mystery party for New Years, and much of our conversation centered around that. I immediately felt invited and involved into this vibrant and engaging community.

As we said our goodbyes, everyone asked if we were "going to the Five."

"Why is everyone going back to the five o'clock service?" I asked Jenny. "Isn't it just going to be the same message?"

"No, it's usually a different pastor and a different message," she answered. "Do you want to go?"

"What time does it end?" I asked, wondering if I could still make the seven o'clock service at my church.

"Usually 6:30, I think," she replied.

If I dip out quickly, I can still make it to my church on time, I thought. *Plus I get to spend more time with Jenny. This will be great.*

At the five o'clock service, another pastor preached, a guy named Drew. Sitting in the middle of the front row, however, was Jurgen. He was the loudest person clapping and cheering Drew on. I also saw other pastors I had met, all of them cheering, taking notes, and fully engaged.

As I had been at the Richard Foster conference, I was struck by the contrast between this and my church, where I had never seen the senior pastor watch any other pastor from the audience. If my pastor was there, he was preaching. If he wasn't preaching, he wasn't in the building, because he had a better opportunity somewhere else. It struck me that what I was seeing at C3, and had seen at the Renovaré conference, was the better way to raise up leaders. Someone in leadership willingly gave up a good opportunity to allow someone else to step up into it, and then walked with them through that. Then I remembered my words to Richard Foster at lunch—that if I found a church that operated the way I saw his conference operate, I didn't think I'd ever leave. As I watched Drew preach and Jurgen cheer him on, I had a strong suspicion that I had found that church, and found my home.

I started getting involved at C3 and attending a variety of their events, including a Tuesday morning men's prayer meeting that was unlike any men's group I had ever seen. It was filled with men who were great leaders in their careers, great husbands and fathers in their homes, and great friends in their communities. Almost no one was weird or socially awkward, and the man who led the group, Dr. Matt, who happened to be the head of the California State Board of Chiropractors, was one of the most encouraging men I'd ever met. I was so impressed with the caliber of men in that group. I felt like I found a group of guys who could be mentors for various areas of my life where I needed guidance.

Jenny and I started seeing each other almost every day and going to church together every Sunday. On our third Sunday, Jurgen preached in the morning, but a man named Jon preached at night. His style was different than the other pastors I had seen so far, and I didn't like it. At discipleship school, I had been taught by men who surgically dissected Scripture, making the Bible come alive so much more powerfully than I could on my own. Jon had a very different style than what I had come to consider good preaching, and I made several negative judgments against him almost immediately.

That night, I found out there was a two-day event called Freedom Conference happening the upcoming weekend where a pastor named Mike Connell, who was known for deliverance and healing, would be preaching. My leg was still a source of constant pain, and I wanted it to be gone. I really believed that the conference was where I was going to get breakthrough, so Jenny and I signed up together.

The Power to Change

The conference was unlike anything I had ever experienced. Mike Connell taught on several areas related to the topic of deliverance. I had heard other people talk about deliverance in the past, and had judged some of them as being overly spiritual or weird. There was nothing weird about Mike. He was extremely clear and sensible. Several times, he invited the audience up if they needed prayer in the area he was addressing. I went up to release unforgiveness and break off emotional and spiritual bonds with people I had slept with in the past.

In the last session of the conference, Mike invited people up for healing, and I went. Several pastors stood at the front praying for the crowds of people that came forward, but I really wanted to have Mike pray for me. I had been in pain now for eighteen months, and had spent close to a hundred thousand dollars on treatment¬. I didn't need some second-string amateur praying for me—I needed an expert.

I was next in line to be prayed for by Pastor Mike when I felt a tap on my shoulder. It was Pastor Jon. "I can pray for you," he offered.

Of all the people. I didn't think Jon was qualified to preach, let alone pray for me. I wanted to say, "No thanks, I'll wait" but I didn't want to be rude. Jon and his wife were the campus pastors, and I had just started going to this church. "Thank you," I said, but internally, I was so upset. I didn't even listen as he prayed—I just wanted it to be over. I wondered if I could sneak back into line without him seeing me, but I worried if he did, he'd know I thought his prayer wasn't good enough, and I didn't want him to be offended.

While I was being prayed for, I saw Mike Connell finish praying and walk backstage. I'd missed my chance to be healed. That was the whole reason I had come to the conference. I was so angry, but I didn't want to let Jenny or anyone else know, because I didn't want to seem ungrateful.

About a month later, the church held a series of classes called "DNA Gifts of the Spirit." The first evening session was split into two parts—the first focusing on the gift of tongues and the second on the gift of healing. I found out that Dr. Matt, the man who led the men's prayer group, was going to be speaking on healing and praying for people at the end of the session.

Though my pain had only continued to get worse over time, whenever I prayed, I felt like breakthrough was right around the corner. Jenny and I signed up for the class. I was excited for Dr. Matt to pray for me. At the session, Dr. Matt and Pastor Jon spoke. Pastor Jon talked about how he had been prayed for when he was in the hospital with kidney failure and had been miraculously healed. Though his story was impressive, Dr. Matt was actually a doctor and healed people for a living. I knew from Tuesday mornings that he was also an incredible prayer warrior, and I believed in him.

At the end of the session, Jon and Matt stood on opposite ends of the stage and people lined up for prayer. I was next to be prayed for by Dr. Matt when I looked over and saw that Jon's line was empty. As I looked in his direction, Jon made eye contact with me. I quickly looked away, but a moment later, felt a tap on my shoulder. You've got to be kidding. I looked up to see Pastor Jon standing next to me, smiling one of the sincerest smiles I think I'd ever seen.

"Can I pray for you?" he asked, motioning for me to follow him over to the other side of the room.

Words cannot fully express how I felt in that moment—somewhere between utter frustration, exhaustion for having this pain for so long, deeply touched, and convicted that though I really didn't want him to pray for me, Jon was sincerely trying to help.

As we walked together over to the other side of the auditorium, I felt God say, "*Do you really think it's him who's going to heal you, or do you think I can use anybody?* "

That thought hit me hard. Had I really been that religious that I thought God had only specially qualified those who I thought were worthy?

God, I'm sorry, I prayed immediately. *I believe You can use anybody. In fact, You have a long history of using the least likely of all.*

Jon prayed for me. It was a simple but heartfelt prayer. At the end of it, he asked me to do something I hadn't been able to do since before the pain started. I hadn't taken my medication that day, because if I received healing, I wanted to know that it was real. I bent down in a position that would normally send an excruciatingly painful shock through my leg and lower back. Nothing happened. I knelt down on the ground and sat in between my heels, a position I couldn't get into without medication since I had practiced yoga years before. No pain.

My mind raced. *There's no way.* From kneeling on the floor, sitting between my ankles, I leaned back all the way until my back, head, and shoulders were flat on the floor. I was trying to feel pain, and there was none. It was completely gone.

I told Jon. I think he was as surprised as I was. It was a miracle healing that came through a man I had judged. The thing that I "needed to let go of" wasn't my pain—it was my religiousness and my lack of faith in how God could move.

CHAPTER 15:
Planted to Grow

As Jenny and I grew in our relationship, I continued to get more involved at C3. Through the Tuesday morning prayer meeting, Sunday services, and serving, I found myself surrounded by incredible men—great husbands, fathers, leaders, teachers, and friends—who generously and willingly shared their wisdom and learning with me. Through their example and input, I started to grow more rapidly than I ever had before in every area of my life.

In my relationship with Jenny, conversations that in previous relationships had been hard were easy and natural. I started being able to see a future with her. One night as we were talking, I was gazing into her eyes, and I saw her differently than I ever had before¬. I realized that she was the most beautiful girl I had ever seen, and I had a feeling that I was going to spend the rest of my life with her. As we served together at church, I got to see her heart for others as she counseled and prayed for them, which bolstered my confidence that she would be a great wife and mother.

Through serving, I also started making new friends. One of those friends was Tom Foster. Tom invited me onto his team for Emerge, the church's men's conference. From the promo video, the conference looked like a three-day, high-energy, über-testosterone-filled, guy-fest campout—not something I'd ever willingly sign up for. From a relational standpoint, though, I knew I'd regret not going. There were going to be some great speakers, and it would be an opportunity to make some new friends and strengthen relationships with the men I was getting to know. If there was anything I didn't want to do, I could find a way to duck out.

In addition to great teaching and time for connection, a large component of Emerge centered around competition. Truthfully, though I'd been able to fake my way through it in life, I had never been a team player. Some of that had to do with fear of rejection and unworthiness, a residual result of childhood, and some of it had to with a deep fear of really committing to being a part of something.

Tom is a man's man, about 6'5" and built like a tank. He had been a captain in the Coast Guard for twenty years, and looked like he could probably wrestle a great white to the ground if he was really pressed. I was honored to be a part of his team, but really didn't see myself dominating the field games, and planned on avoiding participating in that part of the conference. When I tried to explain to Tom that I wasn't really the "rah, rah, rah" football-and-beer guy, however, he didn't even acknowledge my excuse. He simply told me—in a kind, not a forceful, arrogant, or condescending way—that I'd be participating.

Tom and the other leaders explained that the heart behind the competition element of the conference was to build up men to be men—to compete, but in a way that builds up, not tears down. It's about competing with men who want you to grow as much as they want to win—men with hearts that say, "I want the guy who just lost to me to grow and outdo what I just did." This kind of competition is fostered by leaders who lead with the hope that their protégés will surpass their best. It's part of a culture of men so bent on legacy that they've developed the heart of fathers, mining the gold out of the ones they're leading.

I saw this style of leadership modeled throughout the conference, and it was so different to what I had ever encountered in life, even in the church culture I had been exposed to in the past. Tom exemplified this in the way he kept encouraging me in a strong but gentle way.

I thought back to my first team experience playing soccer as a child in Vancouver and saw how I had always opted out when things didn't go my way. I have never been an "all in" guy in my heart. I never submitted under authority. Sure, I would comply to get what I wanted, but never submit in my heart. I didn't see how giving up my "freedom" could ever result in growth. When it came to God, I thought if I really went "all in" and got "sold out," everything great about me would die. I'd somehow lose myself to something that wasn't really me. Now I was surrounded by men who were literally the best men I had ever met, successful in every way, and they were clearly "all in."

I made the decision that I was going to be different. Even though I didn't see the road ahead of me, I was going to commit to participating with everything I had. And I really believe God met me there. I showed up physically in ways I didn't know I had in me. I also opened up relationally and submitted to leadership under Tom in a way I don't think I had ever done. As a result, I experienced a feeling of connection and belonging with the guys around me in a way I never had before.

Over the course of the conference, I felt another tugging on my heart. By this time, Jenny and I had been together for three months, and I knew I wanted to marry her. The conference was the last week of March. Her birthday was coming up the second week of May, and I thought it would be the perfect day to ask her. I wanted it to be a surprise, and to do something elaborate.

After deciding to show up fully at the conference, I couldn't wait to see how far that attitude would take me in other areas of life, including marriage. When I was in my twenties, there was a popular tee-shirt with a bride and groom and the words "Game Over" on it. When I saw it, I thought rhetorically, *How true is that?* I had always looked at commitment as a loss of freedom—that if I really committed to something or somebody, I would limit possibility in my life. At that point, I spent most of my time hanging out with other guys who were stuck in a life of no commitments, and we would talk about how marriage was the end of freedom. The men I was now hanging out with at C3 were completely different. Most of them were married, and I saw that they were experiencing greater levels of freedom in growth than one could ever achieve as a single person. Watching them, I became more and more excited about marriage and a future with Jenny.

My mom had been saving the diamond from my grandmother's engagement ring for me, and I designed a setting. I also designed a canvas cabana I was going to set up at the beach for our engagement dinner. I invited our closest friends and Jenny's twin sister to come and celebrate with us after I proposed. Finally, I called her father and asked for her hand in marriage.

The day of the proposal arrived. I built the canvas cabana, and a friend helped me build a platform and floor out of recycled palette wood. We brought these, along with a large teak dining table, down to a small private beach about a mile from my house. I set the table with six dozen long stem white roses, placed lanterns around the outside, and ordered dinner from an incredible Italian restaurant we both loved.

Jenny suspected a surprise, but had no idea what was in store. We parked and walked down to the beach just in time for sunset. She was delighted by the scene I had set for us, but really thought this was all for her birthday. We ate and talked, watching the setting sun, and then I started to tell her a story about the ancient Jewish custom of Erusin, or betrothal.

"You know, in ancient Israel, when a man was interested in marrying a woman, he'd go to her father and buy his permission to sit with his daughter for dinner in a tent. They called this tent a *'huppa."* The man would pour a glass of wine and then pass it to the woman, and if she took it she was saying, 'I'll marry you.' So . . . I called your dad this week and asked him if he would give me permission . . ."

Joy and surprise filled Jenny's eyes as I got down on one knee. When I pulled the little box from my pocket and opened it to reveal a beautiful ring, tears began streaming down her face.

"Will you marry me?"

"Yes!" she screamed, leaping up from her chair to hug me.

At that moment, about ten of our friends emerged from behind shrubs at the top of the hill and came down to celebrate with us.
I had never been so sure about someone in my life. The relationship so far had been almost effortless. All the time spent in practicing healthy intimacy, writing her letters before we met, and building strong relationships with other men for support really paid off. Now it was real—I was going to share my life with someone and build a family and home together, something I had always wanted, but doubted if I would ever be worthy of or qualified for. I didn't have those doubts anymore, though. I was so excited to start building a life together.

Two days after we got engaged, Jenny called me in the middle of the day and asked me out to dinner. She said there were some things from her past that she really needed to talk to me about. Although I had told her part of my story, I hadn't yet told her everything about my past. I wasn't trying to hide it—we had only known each other five months, and the opportunity hadn't yet presented itself. I was a little nervous, but I thought that this might be the opportunity.

We met at a crowded restaurant, but were able to get a quiet booth in a corner. Jenny shared with me some things about her past relationships that were heavy, but in my mind, nothing as bad as what I had been through. She had been worrying that after this conversation, I would want to take the ring back and break off the engagement. After hearing the details of her story, however, I didn't love her less—I loved her so much more. I shared my past with her as well, and with everything out on the table, and neither one of us wanting to run screaming for the door, I knew that we'd be able to get through anything that could possibly come up in our marriage.

Over the next five months, we planned the wedding together, I finished renovations to my house to prepare for Jenny to move in, and we went through premarital counseling with a couple from the church, Matt and Mikala. Our first session with them reviewed an assessment we had both taken as a prerequisite to counseling. Part of the assessment was a twelve-category compatibility survey looking at areas like beliefs around finance, raising kids, conflict resolution, etc.—things that are important to be on the same page about. Matt said he had never seen a couple so compatible in eleven out of the twelve categories on the assessment. He said we were within four points of one another. But, he said he had never seen a couple with a larger point spread on the last category, comfortability with change. Jenny was 8% comfortable with change, and I was 98% comfortable. Matt said that this was the one category where it wasn't necessarily important to be perfectly compatible, but to have great communication. Matt said that he and his wife were similar in that regard, and predicted that Jenny would really help ground me when my head was in the clouds, and that I would make her life a whole lot more exciting.

We had both been saving and working at a high capacity for years and decided to split the costs for the wedding. We didn't necessarily want a huge wedding, but both of us had large communities of friends and family that we wanted to invite. We were limited to 170 guests at the venue we chose, and each could commit to putting in $35,000.

About three weeks out from the wedding, Jenny called me on a Wednesday evening. She had just crunched the numbers and realized that we were $10,000 over budget. Neither of us had more money we could contribute, and I could tell she was starting to freak out.

"There's nothing we can do right now, so let's pray that God would figure it out," I told her.

I pulled my car over, and we prayed specifically that God would find the money for us. Less than two hours later, I got a text from a long-time client. He had a last-minute project he needed finished in two days, and the budget was exactly $10,000. I accepted the offer and immediately called Jenny. I couldn't believe it—never had I seen God answer a prayer so specifically, and so quickly.

Everything else leading up to the wedding came together just like that. We were extended on the wedding cost, and without even asking, my parents and best man offered to pay for our honeymoon. Pastor Jon, who had prayed when my leg got healed, officiated our ceremony. (The irony of that still amazes me.) And high-paying projects came in at exactly the right time, and in the right way, so that I was able to be fully present with Jenny while making enough money to set us up well into our marriage.

We had a tough time narrowing the guest list. Both of us had so many people we loved and who had played a big part in our lives. We looked at each person and asked, "Is this someone who is going to support our marriage and who we want in our lives in the future?" That was a tough question to answer, but it helped really bring us together as a couple before the wedding.

We had both been to weddings officiated by pastors who took the ceremony hostage, and though we weren't really worried about Jon, we talked to him about it. I had been so offended when Christian friends had pushed their faith on me, and the last thing I wanted to do was make our guests feel like we had invited them with an agenda. Both of us had spent a lifetime waiting for this day, and we wanted it just to be a celebration of our love for one another and for the people who had been with us through the journey.

At last, the day arrived. Our wedding was like something out of a fairy tale. We were married in a beautiful white gazebo on the shore of a heart-shaped lake. Jenny arrived in a carriage drawn by two white horses. She looked so gorgeous, and was so giddy with joy and anticipation at the altar that she was literally bouncing and smiling from ear to ear.

As I looked into her eyes, I thought, Only God could have done this. Where I was, what I'd done, what had been done to me—I had disqualified myself from this moment a hundred times over, but somehow God had fully and truly redeemed it all. I no longer felt like an outsider looking in at my life. I was right here, in such a state of joy I could barely contain it. Would I take this woman to have and to hold, in sickness and in health, for richer or for poorer, as long as we both shall live? Absolutely.

The ceremony was short and sweet. Gia, my friend who introduced us, sang. It was perfect. Every detail, from the meal to the desserts, the DJ at the reception, and the decor was exactly what we wanted. There was no drama with the guests. In fact, every single person commented that they could feel the love.

My parents sent us to Kauai for our honeymoon. It was a perfect start to our marriage. One thing we weren't prepared for, though, was what happens next—embarking on the sexual part of our relationship. When we were dating, we were both honest about our past sexual relationships. I had had many more relationships and encounters than Jenny—to say I had been a slut would be a gross understatement. Jenny had had three long-term relationships and had never had a one-night stand. But we had both done all the hard work on ourselves beforehand, and had committed to doing this relationship right, so we didn't have sex before marriage. Yet neither of us had given much thought to what it would be like to come together sexually under a union that had been blessed by God.

I found that sex under the covenant of marriage could not be more different than what I had done in the past, which was effectively masturbating in somebody and allowing that to masquerade as physical intimacy. Because that had been my experience, and I was quite experienced, sex in our marriage initially was awkward. I didn't know what to do, and I didn't want to do it wrong, or in a way that she would feel anything less than loved and adored.

Thankfully, we communicated openly, were patient with one another, and eventually began to experience the joy that I believe God intended us to have with one another. Our initial awkwardness didn't prevent us from moving forward, didn't prevent the growth of our family, and didn't stifle growth in emotional connection and love for one another. It actually facilitated growth in bringing up things that we may not have wanted to bring up on our own volition.

The day after we flew home from Hawaii, I had to fly out with a client to a trade show in New York. New York was one of my favorite cities to visit when I was single, and I often added a week to the end of a work trip to enjoy the city. But Jenny made me promise to fly right home at the end of this trip.

The trade show finished better than expected, and we celebrated with dinner and a Broadway show. After the show, I went for a walk. All I could think about was how I had to fly home in the morning, and I didn't want to. I wanted to go shopping in SoHo and spend a day at the Met, MoMA, and the Guggenheim. I wanted to eat amazing food. But I was married now, and my wife wanted me home. I was frustrated and started to wonder if it really was "Game Over"—if I'd lost my ability to have spontaneous fun.

I walked from my hotel at Columbus Circle down Seventh Avenue, through Times Square all the way down through Greenwich Village past Houston where 7th Ave. becomes Varick. Then a thought hit me and I stopped.

Do I really want to go shopping by myself, spend days at museums by myself, and go eat amazing food by myself? Is that what I'm upset about? Is that what I really want?

It suddenly hit me hard that these were not what I wanted at all. I wanted to share my life with Jenny. I didn't want to be living life by myself and for myself anymore. I wanted to share my life with her and let her share hers with me. I wanted to go home. I missed my wife.

I called her and told her what had happened and how much I missed her. I realized that there was going to be a lot of adjustment, but I was excited about the challenges ahead and coming out the other side.

When I got back home from New York, we decided to start trying for a baby. Jenny had read up on cycles and the best times to try. One night, she told me that according to her calculations, this was the best chance we had in that cycle. I believe I felt it the moment she became pregnant. There was a rush of energy, a feeling I had never felt before. I didn't say anything, because I didn't want to seem weird, but I knew. New Year's Eve, she took a pregnancy test. As we were preparing to receive guests at our first New Year's Eve party as a couple, she pulled me aside and told me that I was going to be a daddy.

I can't describe the joy I felt in that moment. Tears immediately and powerfully flowed down my face. I had wanted to be a father my whole adult life, but with everything I had experienced, I wondered if my past had disqualified me, if that dream would ever become a reality. Yet, from the moment I thought I knew to when Jenny confirmed it, I had been praying for a son. I felt a very specific message from God that I couldn't shake.

I'm going to give you a son, but first I'm going to give you a daughter, because I need to grow your heart, your capacity to love in a way that only a daughter can grow.

When Jen told me, I knew we were going to have a girl. I was so happy, but didn't want to tell all the guests at our New Year's Eve party before we had a chance to tell our families. It took everything in me to keep that secret that night.

That week also marked our one-year anniversary and the one-year anniversary of my first week at C3 Church. As I sat in service that Sunday morning, I reflected on what had been the most remarkable year of my life. I had always dreamed of a life like I had, but wondered if it was really possible. I had a life that I truly looked forward to living. I had an incredible wife who was beautiful inside and out. I remembered what George had told me about a lifetime of unpacking our baggage together. I actually looked forward to it, because if what we had experienced so far was any indicator, it was something that was going to bring us even closer. I was going to be a daddy, and I could hardly wait for all the firsts that were going to happen that year. We were in a community of very real people who live in expectancy of God moving, and supported and encouraged one each other in a way that fostered healthy and rapid growth. We had the most generous pastors I had ever met, who not only shared their wisdom in a beautifully transparent way, but also shared their opportunity, because they were far more concerned with growing big people and calling out leadership in the people they pastored than they were about getting applause. And with all of this, I had a peace in my soul unlike anything I had ever felt.

I thought of Psalm 92:13, "Those who are planted in the house of the Lord shall flourish in the courts of our God." I was living proof.

The Power to Change

CHAPTER 16:
Can You Grow a Beard?

As worship started that Sunday morning, I looked around the auditorium where a year before, I had walked in as a stranger. I saw the faces of many who had become my closest friends—ones I considered family. I was so filled with joy, and felt truly connected in a way I never had before.

When worship ended, they ran a video. It was a teaser trailer and call for auditions for a new rock musical the church was producing called *Hero: From Carpenter to King*. Midway through the video, I felt God say, *You're going to play Jesus.*

I had loved musical theatre as a child, spent summers in San Diego's Junior Theatre, and took classes and workshops starting at age three. I loved to sing . . . until an experience at nine years old made me self-concious about my voice. The day before my mom married my stepfather, Nick, who eventually adopted me, I was driving around with him and his best man. They were going over the order of service and I was looking out the window in the back seat singing, as I frequently did.

Suddenly, Nick turned around and snapped, "You'll never sound as good as your mom. Will you please be quiet?".

I knew he was just stressed and probably didn't mean it, but it shut me up, and I became self-conscious about singing in front of people. I started turning down opportunities for roles, and though I knew I had a four-octave range and perfect pitch, I was terrified to open my mouth to sing, even in front of close friends.

In junior high and high school, I had sung for a couple of bands, but I couldn't make eye contact with anyone when I was singing, and could really only perform if I was wasted. In adulthood, I had been invited to a few karaoke parties and forced to go up on stage. I would sing "Bohemian Rhapsody" or "Somebody to Love" and nail it, pitch perfect. People would tell me, "You've got to do something with that voice!" but I'd brush it off and just sing in the shower.

I knew I had to audition for this rock musical, and was supposed to play the lead. But I also knew that the church's plays were Broadway-level productions, and the fear of auditioning was paralyzing to me.

I called Amy, my best friend Frank's wife. Amy and I had known each other since we met at Junior Theatre summer camp when we were eight years old. Amy and Frank's kids had gotten into theatre, and she had become a total stage mom (but not the controlling, weird kind). I couldn't bring myself to sing to her over the phone, so I recorded myself singing three songs— "Phantom of the Opera," "Bohemian Rhapsody," and Stevie Wonder's "Happy Birthday"—and sent them to her over text. I was so nervous I could barely press "send."

Amy got back to me right away. "Wow, you sound great. I really think you need to do 'Happy Birthday.' It's so you. The other songs are good, but you sound like you're trying too hard. 'Happy Birthday' is effortless."

I had known the song since I was a kid, but I printed out the lyrics so I could look at the sheet in case I was nervous. To make things worse, "Happy Birthday" wasn't a hugely popular song and I couldn't find a backing track, so I was going to have to sing acapella.

The night of the audition arrived. I was excited but also so nervous I almost felt like I was going to pass out. There were dozens of people waiting in the lobby, and we got called back in groups of four. I was in one of the last groups to be called.

They led us back to a small room and called us out one by one. Finally, they called my name. As I stood up and reached in my back pocket for my lyric sheet, I felt God say, *"Are you really going to do that? Are you really going to hide behind that thing and bring maybe seventy percent? Your seventy percent is going to look like some other people's one-hundred-fifty percent, and they're not going to know you had any more in you. But you will, and you will regret it till the day you die knowing that you had so much more to bring. Do you really think I don't have your back in this?"*

I took a deep breath and stuffed the paper back in my pocket.

The room was small and lit with bright fluorescent lights. Behind a long table sat the senior pastor, Leeanne, the campus pastor, Becky, the worship pastor, Andy, and the director Steven. They were all staring at me. It was like something out of American Idol, but much, much worse. I stood there in awkward silence.

"What are you going to sing?" Andy asked.

"Stevie Wonder's 'Happy Birthday.'"

"Wow, okay," he replied, surprised. "Do you have a backing track?"

"No. I couldn't find a good one. I'm going to sing acapella."

I could tell from the group's expressions that they weren't sure if what they were about to see and hear might be really good, or really not good.

"Alright, mate, whenever you're ready," Andy encouraged.

I'm doing this, I told myself. God, I know You've got me. Give me the ability to dig deep and don't let me leave anything on the field. Guide my voice and give me presence.

I looked Andy straight in the eye and started singing. I kept eye contact with each of them as I belted out the high notes, and I knew from their expressions that I was killing it.

When I finished, Andy gaped at me in astonishment and asked, "Where have you been?"

"Can you grow a beard?" Becky piped up.

"Uh, yeah, I can grow a beard," I nodded.

Leeanne chimed in. "Um . . . this is going to sound a little strange, but how would you feel about being bloodied and beaten on stage in your underwear in front of seven hundred people, several nights in a row, possibly while singing a rock ballad . . . actually probably… definitely while singing a rock ballad?"

I knew what she was asking, but I felt I'd already done the hardest part—overcoming my fear and singing directly to people whose opinion meant the world to me. And I'd been able to look them straight in the eyes and really give my best performance.

"I'd be honored to do it," I said enthusiastically. "Thank you so much."

Over the next several months, we practiced a few nights a week. There wasn't a night that I went out on stage without fear, but as I kept stepping out, I started to outgrow the fear that had crippled me most of my life and build the confidence that God really did have my back.

The night of our first show, I threw my back out carrying the three-hundred-pound cross. Prayer and adrenaline carried me through the performance that night, but when I woke up the following day I couldn't even walk. I called my friend and chiropractor Dr. Matt, and he came in to his office to adjust me. He took X-rays, and I could tell from his expression that he was worried. He prayed over me as well. I also called my friend Jim, who was playing the devil in the show, and also happened to be a wellness coach who specialized in a dynamic stretching technique (DCT). His fiancée Isa was a massage therapist. They both came over and prayed over me, asking God to work supernaturally, and also used their talents to work on my physical body. As they prayed and worked on me, I felt a shift. When I got up off the floor, I felt no pain.

That night and the next, I had two back-to-back performances at six and eight. I made it through all four shows, carrying the cross, singing, and dancing with no pain. The pain never returned. The following Monday, Dr. Matt told me that when I came in he had been worried that I had damaged my back so badly that I would need surgery, but miraculously on Monday when he checked me, he couldn't even feel where there had been injury.

❧

Around the same time as the play, I went to the church's annual men's retreat, Emerge. I was on Tom Foster's team again, and this year I brought a small army of guys in recovery. After being so impacted by the conference the year before, I couldn't wait to see what this year had in store for me and for them.

The first night, the team captains were called up on stage. The year before, Mike Clark had captained the Red Team to victory, but this year that team was being captained by a guy named Jeff Forbes, who had just become a Christian at the conference the year before. As I looked at all the team captains, I noticed that none of them were pastors. All the church pastors were on teams, but none of them were captains. All of them had submitted under the authority of men they had raised up.

I had heard Christian friends of mine talk about "being submitted under a pastor's authority." I thought that was some weird religious term. What did that even mean? At my previous church, I didn't even know the pastor. Why would I submit to someone with whom I didn't have a relationship? I had always been a nine-toes-in, one-toe-out guy anyway. I had never been all in. I had never been planted anywhere. I had thought that putting down roots meant limiting opportunity, destroying spontaneity, and losing freedom. When I came to C3, though, all that changed. I had actually put down roots, gone all in, and submitted under a pastor's guidance. I didn't do it out of religious obedience—I did it out of love.

I hadn't even realized what had happened until that night as I watched the men on stage at the men's retreat. I knew Jeff. I saw his life turn around, saw him grow, and saw him step into leadership—not just at church, but in his life as a husband, father, friend, and worker among workers. I also had seen all those other men grow, just as I had, under great leadership by pastors who had laid down their lives to raise us up.

In the year that had passed since the first men's conference, I had gotten engaged and married, and my wife and I had gotten pregnant with a baby girl. I had starred in a rock musical, stepping out of thirty years of fear. I had experienced miraculous healing, became a respected leader in the church, and had taken greater leadership roles in my community, recovery fellowship, and career. I had a suspicion, though, that God was just getting started, and that the best years of my life lay ahead.

CHAPTER 17:
The Promise in the Process

September 16th, 2015, a little over ten months after Jenny and I were married, my daughter Ella was born. When God told me He wanted to grow my heart and was giving me a daughter, I had no idea I would ever be capable of that kind of love.

The pregnancy and birth were not without challenges, though. Jenny wanted to have a natural birth, but a few weeks prior to her due date we discovered that Ella was what they call "frank breech." A frank-breech baby has its buttocks towards the birth canal and its legs extended out straight in front of its head. Our conversation about the birth plan changed towards options, and the possibility of those options not working, and a C-section being necessary. The only option they gave us that would allow Jenny to have the all-natural birth that she wanted was through a process called external cephalic version (ECV), or version for short. In a version, doctors attempt to externally maneuver the baby into proper head-down birthing position at thirty-seven weeks gestation. The process is extraordinarily painful for the mother, has the risk of serious complications, and is rarely successful (5-7%) in the case of a frank breech. But Jenny wanted to go ahead with it.

As the doctors and nurses began the procedure, I held Jenny's hand. she squeezed so hard that her nails punctured my palm. I would have given anything to take her place and take the pain away. The first attempt appeared successful, but just as the doctor removed his hand from Jenny's belly, Ella flipped back around. All of that pain, and it failed.

I prayed under my breath, "God I know You gave Your back for our healing. Please, please, please make this work."

The doctors explained that these types of breeches were very difficult to turn, and that they were only going to make three attempts at most. If they felt Jenny couldn't take it or the baby was in danger, they would stop after two. Did Jenny want to go on? She nodded, covered in sweat. I could barely stand to see her in so much pain.

The second attempt ended the same way, with apparent success and then failure. The doctors were willing to try for three, but I could tell by their expressions that they weren't hopeful. I asked Jenny if she really wanted to go through that again. She did.

I was nervous, but wanted to support her. *Stay strong, Morgan. Encourage her.*

At this point I had no idea what to pray for, and I told God that. As the doctors began the procedure again, I squeezed Jenny's hand, closed my eyes, and began to pray in tongues. I prayed with everything in me. If she wasn't backing down, neither was I. I had exhausted all my ideas of what to pray for, but as I entered into that prayer I didn't understand, I felt something shift. Ella moved. She moved into perfect birthing position, and she stayed put.

Cheers, tears, and laughter erupted in the room. I hugged Jenny. She was so strong. My wife is a warrior. The doctors wiped the sweat off her belly and bruising began to show. I marveled at her strength and commitment to seeing her vision of a natural birth through.

The Power to Change

In San Diego, we have a world-renowned birthing center at UCSD Medical Center. Jenny wanted to have Ella there from the beginning of her pregnancy, but it was not without complication. Jenny had back labor, which is extraordinarily painful. Her labor was also long, and by the time she wanted drugs to ease the pain, she was too far along to get them. Then, when Ella was born, because of a blurred x-ray, the doctors thought she had a lung infection. They took our baby girl out of our arms to the neonatal intensive care unit (NICU) and put her on a five-day round of antibiotics. By the time the error in the x-ray was discovered, we were committed to seeing the five days of antibiotics out. Absolutely nothing went according to our plan, but thankfully by being at the hospital, we had great specialists who prepared us to finally bring Ella home.

Soon after we came home, however, Jenny and I ended up in a conflict over me attending a Wednesday night recovery meeting. This meeting was one I had helped start with my friend, Tyla, soon after having my transformative experience with my sponsor, Mark. From the beginning, I served there, speaking, leading 12 Step workshops, and guiding men through the process that helped lead me to God. For me, there is something uniquely therapeutic about being able to serve a person with whom I have no legal or familial connection—to be able to freely give of my time, as others had done for me, and take the things the enemy had intended for evil and watch God use them for good. I was deeply committed to this group, and Jenny knew not to book anything for us from six to nine on Wednesdays, because if we were in town, I would be there.

The Wednesday meetings are usually lively, with people are constantly praising the miraculous work God has done in their lives. I was especially excited to share the joy of the birth of my daughter with the group. Ella was born on a Wednesday, and I assumed Jenny would be totally okay with me going to my meeting the following Wednesday night. I was wrong. We got in a huge fight. She said she needed me at home. I backed down, but said that the following Wednesday I would do whatever I needed to do to get her the support she needed, because I felt I needed to go to my meeting to get filled up.

The next Wednesday came. Several times during the week prior, I had asked Jenny if she needed anything for the time I'd be gone at the meeting, but she hadn't told me anything. As I was about to shower and prepare to leave, I asked again, but still received no response. I shut the door to the bathroom and thought, This isn't good.

As I got dressed, Jenny asked with disdain, "Are you really going to leave us?"

"I'm only leaving for a couple of hours," I answered. "I have been doing my best to show up for you and Ella, and I really need to get filled up myself. I asked you several times if you needed help, if you needed me to do anything before, and you didn't ask for anything. And you didn't tell me what you needed."

"I need *you!*"

"That's not fair."

"*This* isn't fair. You have a two-week-old daughter and a wife who both need you, *and you're leaving!*"

"I have to go."

As I walked out, I felt torn. I thought I was doing the right thing in taking care of myself, ultimately so I could take care of both Jenny and Ella better, but those words pierced my heart and I felt conflicted knowing I was needed at home.

I had my pastor Jurgen's phone number in my phone. I had never used it for myself, but in this moment I really needed some advice. I texted him: "I'm not sure you're available right now, but I could really use some husband advice."

My phone rang immediately. I told Jurgen what had happened.

"You did exactly the right thing," Jurgen assured me. "But listen. You have a beautiful, wonderful wife. Right now Jenny is feeling like a deflated balloon, the least attractive she's ever felt. She's recovering from the birth, and you two can't be intimate for several more weeks. Meanwhile you're lavishing attention on little Ella, and Jenny's wondering if your love tank has anything left for her. The truth is, your love tank hasn't been divided—it's been expanded. I know you love Jenny more than ever. When you go home tonight, you just need to reassure her that she's still your number-one girl."

Everything Jurgen said was true, and I just assumed Jenny already knew it. How couldn't she know? She had been a fearless warrior. She was the mother of my child. I thought I knew what love for her was before, but it had grown infinitely more than I had even thought possible. Of course, I would tell her—I wanted her to know!

Jurgen and I ended up talking for almost an hour. He told me what the early days of his marriage were like, sharing intimate and embarrassing details with me that paralleled some challenges that Jenny and I had faced. How could he have possibly known so specifically what to say that would minister to me so powerfully in my moment of need if God hadn't shown him?

When I went home after the meeting, I felt filled up, and was excited to talk with Jenny. As I spoke, she melted into my arms.

"I love you so much," she sobbed.

"I love you more than words could ever express," I replied.

I don't believe anyone comes into marriage as a finished work. I know Jenny and I are a work in progress, but I'm so grateful for our pastors Jurgen and Leeanne, who have been mentors and role models to us. Their willingness to openly share the struggles they went through as a young married couple, as well as the wisdom they've gotten navigating marriage and parenting the past twenty-seven years, have given us both comfort and much-needed direction, especially as our family has grown. When Ella was twenty months old, my wife gave birth to a beautiful baby boy we named Jack. Jack means "God is gracious," and He truly is.

We have continued to face challenges and experience breakthroughs. In the process, I've discovered that the greatest breakthroughs come through the greatest struggles. I don't know if I thought at some point life would be easier. Some things have gotten much easier. My self-destructive impulses rarely rear their ugly heads. Other things though have gotten much harder. The greater the growth, the greater the challenge. When I had a small life, I was responsible for no one but myself. I didn't own a company, didn't have a wife or a family, and didn't have to worry about managing a team, investments, bills, and everything else. Life was relatively easy, but it was also very small. As I have been stretched to a bigger life and a larger calling, I have come up against myself, other people, and God over and over again. As I've continued to walk forward, even in pain, even in doubt, even when I couldn't see an inch in front of me, I have found that God's been with me every step of the way.

The past five years, I have been asked to play Jesus in Hero. What an incredible honor it has been to have that role. It has forced me to really consider Jesus through a very different lens. It has grown my faith and my understanding of the gospel by inviting me to look at the world and its people through His eyes. To think that I, who mocked Christians, who once walked out of The Passion of the Christ at the theater, would step into that role with honor and deep gratitude to know Christ better through it still boggles my mind.

Every year, performing the role has had new challenges, not just mentally and emotionally, but also in my physical life and the life of my family. One year, my car was broken into and my wife's car was stolen on the same night. Another year, my dryer caught on fire and I had third-degree burns on both hands and arms two weeks before the show. I took a three-hundred-pound cross to the mouth, splitting my lip open and almost knocking out my two front teeth. I lost my voice completely after the first show on a day we had three performances, but after a lot of prayer was miraculously able to perform the rest of the night without incident. I was told that being on the front lines of ministry was tough.

The Power to Change

It is, but God is also there so profoundly, and He has always restored in one way or another the things that were lost or damaged.

For over four years now, I have also been a captain for a team of over forty men at the Emerge men's conference. To grow from one who was never a team player to a team captain is, to me, nothing short of a miracle. I have seen God move powerfully in the lives of the men I have been blessed with the honor of leading.

Leading a team at the conference also prepared me to lead teams in the marketplace. For three years, I served as Executive Creative Director of a prominent creative agency, working with several of the largest companies in the world. This year, I co-founded a creative agency of my own.

I never imagined that I would be able to tell my story without shame. The first time I was asked to share a short testimony at church, I prayed and asked God where He wanted me to go with it. Should I stick to the safe testimony I was used to telling in recovery meetings, that I was a teenage drug addict and God delivered me? When I asked God, the answer came back clear as day¬: "If you censor what I've done in your life, you will censor what I can do through your life."

I knew I had to tell the full story, but I knew there were parts of it my parents didn't even know, and if I was going to tell that story from stage and have it live on the internet in perpetuity, I would have to share it with them first. I did, and it was wonderful—there were tears and laughter, and I felt an even greater closeness to my family. Not only did I not have anything left to hide, I started to see the fullness of that promise of Genesis 50:20, that what the enemy meant for evil, God will use for good. In sharing what I thought was my worst, God has used it for His best, and allowed me to help set people free.

Paul promised in Philippians 1:6 that "(God) who began a good work in you will carry it on to completion until the day of Christ Jesus." Basically, God will finish the work He started in me, but I'll be a work in progress until the day He calls me home to heaven or Christ returns to earth. Until then, I get to rest in the knowing that He's with me and I'm growing. The timing is His, not mine, and I don't have to worry.

I once heard Pastor John Bevere preach on Proverbs 9:10: "The fear of the Lord is the beginning of wisdom." He said that it wasn't about living in fear of God, but being terrified to live without Him. He said that practicing the fear of the Lord was simply making a decision to live as if the Bible were true, whether it made sense or not. When I believed that the Bible was nonsense, a book followed by adults who believed in fairy tales, my life lay in ruins. When I started believing in God and lining up my own life with the Bible, I started to flourish, as did those around me. This alignment was not simply a matter of following principles in my own effort, however. Trusting God gave me access to power I never had before.

Looking back at my alcoholism, I know now that I was thirsty for things you can't drink. The same was true with my desire for sex, control, food, and success. When I finally came to Christ—broken, lost, and willing to be proven wrong—I found the power I had never been able to reach before. It was power to live to the end of any given day, power to have the courage to face the next day, power to love, power to have friends, power to help people, power to be sane, power to stay sober, power to lead.

I live on a much deeper and more significant level than I ever have before, and I am today a fairly creative, relatively sane human being. I don't have secrets. I have a wife, a daughter, and a son whom I love deeply, and who love me back. I am the same man at work as I am at home, at church, and on social media. I have a life I look forward to waking up to, and when my head hits the pillow at night, there's nothing keeping me up. None of that was possible before I met Jesus. I thank God He gave me the *power to change*.

The Power to Change